simply beautiful

beaded jewelry

50 QUICK AND EASY PROJECTS

heidi boyd

NORTH LIGHT BOOKS
CINCINNATI, OHIO
www.artistsnetwork.com

10   09   08   07   06   5   4   3   2   1

Distributed in Canada by Fraser Direct
100 Armstrong Avenue
Georgetown, ON, Canada L7G 5S4
Tel: (905) 877-4411

Distributed in the U.K. and Europe by David &
Charles
Brunel House, Newton Abbot, Devon, TQ12 4PU,
England
Tel: (+44) 1626 323200, Fax: (+44) 1626 323319
Email: mail@davidandcharles.co.uk

Distributed in Australia by Capricorn Link
P.O. Box 704, S. Windsor, NSW 2756 Australia
Tel: (02) 4577-3555

Library of Congress Cataloging-in-Publication Data

Boyd, Heidi
  Simply beautiful beaded jewelry / Heidi Boyd.-- 1st
ed.
      p. cm.
  Includes index.
  ISBN-13: 978-1-58180-774-5
  ISBN-10: 1-58180-774-0
1. Beadwork. 2. Jewelry making. I. Title.
  TT860.B688 2006
  745.594'2--dc22

                              2005026360

Editor: Jessica Gordon
Designers: Karla Baker and Kathy Gardner
Layout Artist: Kathy Gardner
Production Coordinator: Greg Nock
Photographers: Christine Polomsky, Tim Grondin
Stylists: Jan Nickum, Nora Martini

F•W PUBLICATIONS, INC.

metric conversion chart

TO CONVERT	TO	MULTIPLY BY
Inches	Centimeters	2.54
Centimeters	Inches	0.4
Feet	Centimeters	30.5
Centimeters	Feet	0.03
Yards	Meters	0.9
Meters	Yards	1.1
Sq. Inches	Sq. Centimeters	6.45
Sq. Centimeters	Sq. Inches	0.16
Sq. Feet	Sq. Meters	0.09
Sq. Meters	Sq. Feet	10.8
Sq. Yards	Sq. Meters	0.8
Sq. Meters	Sq. Yards	1.2
Pounds	Kilograms	0.45
Kilograms	Pounds	2.2
Ounces	Grams	28.4
Grams	Ounces	0.04

ABOUT THE
author

Heidi Boyd is an experienced designer who specializes in creating accessible and elegant projects ideal for the beginning crafter or for anyone who is pressed for time. Her projects have been featured in many of the **BETTER HOMES AND GARDENS** publications, and Heidi has also appeared on **HOME & GARDEN TELEVISION** demonstrating projects from her books.

Look for her three other titles in the Simply Beautiful series, **SIMPLY BEAUTIFUL GREETING CARDS**, **SIMPLY BEAUTIFUL RIBBONCRAFT** and, of course, the wildly successful **SIMPLY BEAUTIFUL BEADING**, a Booklist top ten craft book for 2004. Heidi's other titles include her family-friendly books **WIZARD CRAFTS**, **FAIRY CRAFTS** and **PET CRAFTS**.

After years of working as a project designer and teaching art classes in the Midwest, Heidi now enjoys life near the Maine coast with her husband, their two children and the family dog.

DEDICATED TO...

The soon-to-be newest member of our family, baby Celia, who made her presence known as my constant companion during the making of this book!

acknowledgments · My
deepest gratitude to Jessica Gordon, Christine Polomsky and Karla Baker, who made putting this book together a piece of cake. I continue to be thankful for the support of F+W Publications, Inc., most especially publicity and sales, who work tirelessly to have my books seen and noticed.

contents

introduction

As adults we rarely get the chance for a "do over," but with this book I've been able to do just that. Of course, I'm thrilled with the success of *Simply Beautiful Beading*, but I secretly wished I could have squeezed more jewelry into it. And now, my wish has been granted—in this book I have the fabulous opportunity to focus exclusively on jewelry. Beaded jewelry always catches my eye—I admire my friends' playful collections, discover amazing vintage and designer pieces when relaxing watching television or movies, and take in a huge range of styles when I'm out shopping. All my years of jewelry watching have inspired the projects that fill these pages.

You'll be amazed by how easy, economical and rewarding it is to create beaded jewelry yourself. In the pages that follow, you'll find the basic supplies and techniques you need to get started, plus easy-to-follow steps for each project.

Beyond the pride in answering "I made it myself" to compliments on your beading, there are many other advantages to custom-made jewelry. You can modify designs to suit your personal style, incorporate your favorite colors and adjust the length of any piece. You'll also love gifting your friends and family with original beaded jewelry.

There's never been a better time to become a beading enthusiast. Craft and beading stores are expanding their merchandise to fit the growing market, and there is a spectacular range of beads, crystals, pearls, natural stones and findings to inspire creativity.

Don't hesitate to fill your basket with beads next time you're out shopping. It truly is easy to get started—before long you'll be showcasing your original beaded creations. There's no end to the possible color, bead and stringing combinations. Always keep an eye out for new and interesting designs—even as a new beader you'll be able to go home and enjoy making them yours.

Heidi

beads

To say there is a wide variety of beads on the market is a vast understatement. In this book, I've tried to incorporate as many different varieties as possible, but I've only managed to scratch the surface of what's available. Each time I went shopping I found a new bead that inspired yet another project design. At some point I had to stop; I could have only so many pages in the book. The following is a brief introduction to the different varieties of beads featured in the projects. Please keep in mind that the following photographs are only a sampling; while shopping you'll find color, finish and size variations within each bead type.

Swarovski crystals

types of beads

| SEED BEADS | The smallest beads used in this book, glass seed beads are inexpensive and are available in a wide range of colors. They come in lots of different sizes, and the size of their openings also varies. Make sure you select beads that work with the specified needles, beading cord or thread. If you like uniformity and a wider opening, choose the more expensive Delica brand of seed beads.

| JAPANESE SEED BEADS | The size of Japanese seed beads falls somewhere between seed and *E* beads. They come in different shapes including round, hexagonal or tube. Found exclusively in bead stores, they're distinguished by their unique semi-transparent finish. If you're having trouble locating them, just substitute the desired color of *E* beads or large seed beads. | *E* BEADS | Larger than seed beads, *E* beads also have inherent color and size variations. Faster to string than seed beads, *E* beads are useful for framing and spacing other beads. | BUGLES | Bugle beads are small tubes of glass that come in different lengths and colors. Their openings are close in size to those of seed beads. The shorter the bugle bead, the more light the finished piece will reflect; the longer the bugle, the faster the strand will string together.

Czech glass

| CZECH GLASS | These glass beads get their unique shapes by being pressed into molds. Flowers and leaves are the most common varieties. The advantage of selecting Czech beads is that you can purchase multiples of the same size.

| CRYSTALS | Faceted crystal beads reflect light and add sparkle to any beaded piece. They come in round, cube and bicone shapes. The prices of these beads vary dramatically; the more expensive Austrian varieties such as Swarovski lead crystal are clearer and more reflective than the more economical generic crystal beads.

| FIRE-POLISHED CRYSTALS | These inexpensive crystal beads have been finished with an iridescent coating that adds color to the light refraction. Look for them packaged by color in craft stores, or buy them by the mixed scoop in bead stores.

| FRESHWATER PEARLS | Each of these delicate pearls is uniquely shaped with its own indentations and bumps. They range in size from the smallest rice pearl to an elongated 13mm-long tube shape. The pearls are usually coated with an iridescent colored finish that highlights their inherent irregularities.

dyed freshwater pearls

seed beads

Japanese seed beads

|GLASS PEARLS| These imitation pearls are glass beads covered with a pearlescent coating. They are an affordable and effective costume jewelry alternative to natural pearls.
|SEMIPRECIOUS STONE ROUNDS| These perfectly round beads are formed from semiprecious stones. They're made from a wide variety of stones, from jasper to jade. Because of their perfect roundness they're easily sized on the millimeter chart.
|FACETED STONE BEADS| These highly polished beads are cut from semiprecious stones. A lacework of flat cuts across the front and back of the bead reflects light. Both cushion-shaped jade and round quartz varieties have been used to make earrings and bracelets in this book. |CARVED STONE BEADS| These intricate beads have also been cut from semiprecious stones, this time to create a specific shape such as flowers or animals. The irregularity of the natural stone makes each of these beads unique. |STONE CHIPS| To make these irregular beads, small pieces of semiprecious stone are drilled with a central hole and then highly polished. They can be strung onto a single strand or used individually as focal points.
|DICHROIC GLASS| These beautiful beads feature different colors of glass layered with iridescent coloring to make a unique focal point. |BERRY BEADS| These fun beads are plastic pearls that have been encircled by strands of brightly colored seed beads. Fortunately, you can save yourself the trouble of trying to make them, as they are stocked in some of the national craft chains. |SPACERS| Metal-finished spacer beads come in a variety of shapes and sizes. Keep a selection on hand, as their neutral color makes them the perfect accompaniment to almost all bead types. Sterling silver and silver- and gold-plated spacer beads are longer lasting and more expensive than the base metal varieties.

semiprecious beads

spacer beads

berry beads

dichroic glass beads

size chart

Round beads are easy to measure on a millimeter size chart and are usually packaged with the size printed on the package label or on the container in the bead store. You'll find many of the beads in this book aren't sized because they come from mixed-variety bags or don't have a uniform shape.

BEAD CHART

● ● ● ● ● ●
2mm 3mm 4mm 5mm 6mm 7mm

● ● ● ● ●
8mm 9mm 10mm 12mm 14mm

E beads

stone chips

jewelry findings

Jewelry findings are an integral component of beading. Without the right crimps and clasps, your beadwork will not be wearable. Of course, findings don't serve solely utilitarian purposes. They can also be incredibly decorative—used creatively, they can become a beautiful part of the design. Take a moment to familiarize yourself with the options so that when you're shopping you'll select the right pieces for each project.

general findings

You'll need several basic kinds of findings, such as crimp beads and tubes and head and eye pins, for all your jewelry projects.

| CRIMP BEADS | Crimp beads are used to attach clasps to wire. Select a gold, silver or black finish to match the stringing wire and clasp. | CRIMP TUBES | Crimp tubes come in sizes no. 1 through no. 4. The no. 1 crimps (the smallest) are usually crimped flat, whereas the larger crimps can be crimped twice. | HEAD PINS AND EYE PINS | Head pins have a rounded flat end and are used to create beaded dangles or to link beaded elements. Eye pins are similar to head pins but have an open circle on one end. Head pins and eye pins come in different lengths in gold, silver and copper metal finishes. Elaborate decorative head pins are often harder to manipulate. Fine sterling silver varieties are the easiest to shape. | BEAD CAPS | These are cup-shaped metal beads used to showcase a round bead by framing it on both sides. | SPACER BARS | Spacer bars eliminate twisting problems by allowing two or more strands to lay parallel to each other. | JUMP RINGS | Jump rings are small metal rings that can be opened to hook onto links or jewelry findings and closed to secure a crimp to the end of a strand as part of the clasping system. They are available in different sizes, in metal finishes and in sterling silver. | SPLIT RINGS | A split ring operates just like a small key-chain ring: One end opens laterally, then the charm or chain link slips onto the ring. Split rings provide a more secure connection than jump rings.

clasps

Be sure to select a clasp that matches the scale (size) and style of your beadwork. For instance, an ornate toggle clasp adds interest to a simply strung strand, whereas a small spring clasp better complements a strand of delicate beadwork.

| SPRING CLASP | This is the most common and simplest clasp. A small lever allows it to open and hook onto or unhook from a jump ring or the hole in an accompanying metal tab. | LOBSTER CLASP | The lobster clasp functions like the spring clasp, but the opening allows it to hook onto a larger jump ring or leather loop. | O RING AND TOGGLE CLASP | There are many ornate variations of the O ring and toggle clasp. Each piece is crimped onto the strand end. To fasten, fit the toggle completely through the O ring. | HOOK AND EYE | The hook end simply threads in and out through the eye opening to fasten and unfasten the strand. | FILIGREE CLASPS | In this clasp, a separate folded metal end squeezes flat to slide into the filigree housing. Pinch the metal end together to unfasten the clasp.

earring findings

Earrings provide instant gratification as they're quickly assembled onto findings. You'll find earrings for both pierced and unpierced ears in this book.

| SPRING LEVER | This earring finding opens for placement on the ear and then springs closed for a secure fit. | FRENCH EARWIRE | This earwire is a simple fishhook shape that passes through the ear. | POST EARRINGS | These are the most traditional type of earring base. They are simply posts with backings to secure them. The beads loop through a small ring that hangs below the stud. | HOOP EARRINGS | These are slim wire hoops that are very easy to bead. Purchase the variety that has a smooth wire on one end and a hole in the other.

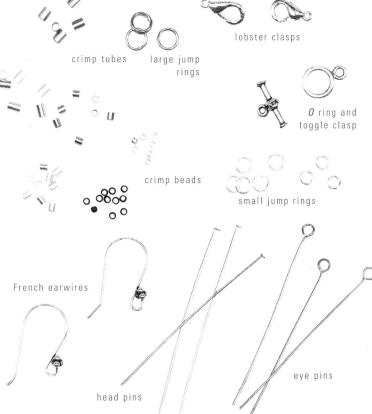

lobster clasps

crimp tubes

large jump rings

O ring and toggle clasp

crimp beads

small jump rings

French earwires

head pins

eye pins

stringing materials

The selection of stringing materials is crucial to the strength and appearance of finished beaded pieces. Follow the material guidelines for each project. You can always change the color, but stick with the specified product type to ensure success. As with findings, the wire or thread you choose to string your piece can have a big impact on the look of the jewelry.

wire and chain

The advantage of beading with wire and chain is that needles or knots aren't needed and beads can be quickly twisted, wrapped or hooked into position. The general rule when buying wire or chain is the higher the gauge number, the thinner the wire, and, conversely, the lower the gauge, the thicker the wire or chain. |**32-GAUGE BEADING WIRE**| A very thin wire, 32-gauge wire easily threads through small seed beads. It's usually available in both gold and silver finishes. Because it's so fine, twists and kinks can quickly cause the wire to break. |**MEMORY WIRE**| Memory wire is resilient coiled wire sold in bracelet, necklace and ring sizes. It's imperative to use either sturdy wire cutters or custom memory wire cutters on this wire. |**26-GAUGE STAINLESS STEEL AND STERLING SILVER WIRE**| Both stainless steel and sterling silver wire have been used in this book. Sterling silver is obviously the more expensive choice, and it is also more pliable than steel. It's worth the added expense if the wire becomes a visible part of the finished piece. Sterling wire can always be polished to restore its sheen, whereas stainless steel has a dull finish. |**BEADALON WIRE**| Beadalon wire is the most commonly used stringing wire because of its strength, availability and ease of use. It has a strong wire core covered with a soft, flexible nylon coating. It's unnecessary to use beading needles with this stringing wire—simply thread the beads onto the rigid end. Beadalon wires come in a multitude of thicknesses and colored finishes, so be careful to select the size indicated on the materials list to ensure that the wire will work with beads, crimps and clasp. |**LINK CHAIN**| Link chain is sold in a variety of thicknesses, from very fine chain to heavy elongated links. The cost of the link chain varies widely depending on the metal content and whether it is plated or solid sterling. All chain can be easily broken into smaller lengths by simply cutting open a single link with wire cutters.

thread and cord

Thread and cord are great options for knotted designs. All the options below come in many colors and sizes. |**LEATHER CORD**| Leather is sold by the yard in jewelry and fabric stores and by packaged lengths in craft stores. Select the cord by color and thickness, gauged in millimeters. |**SILK OR NYLON BEADING THREAD**| This very pliable thread is used primarily for knotted designs. Thread comes in a wide variety of colors and sizes, so make sure you get the right size for the beads you use or your bead holes will eat your knots. |**FIRELINE**| This very fine beading thread has a stiffness that helps ease it through beading needles, and also gives the finished piece strength. |**ELASTICITY 1MM ELASTIC CORD**| This clear heavyweight elastic makes stringing larger beads a breeze. Always treat knotted elastic cord with a dot of glue to help prevent the knot from unraveling. For a more secure connection, this heavyweight variety is substantial enough to be crimped.

gold- and silver-plated Beadalon wire

necklace-, bracelet- and ring-size memory wire

link chain

tools and materials

Of the many specialty tools on the market, only a few are really necessary to get started with beadwork. I strongly suggest purchasing round-nose pliers, chain-nose pliers, crimping pliers, wire cutters and a sharp pair of scissors. You should be able to make all the projects in this book using just these tools.

round-nose pliers

pliers and wire cutters

| ROUND-NOSE PLIERS | Round-nose pliers have two smooth, round, tapered ends that facilitate shaping wire into coils, circles or loops. | CHAIN-NOSE PLIERS | Chain-nose or needle-nose pliers are commonly used in wire jewelry projects. They're perfect for holding the jewelry while wire ends get wrapped. Serrated pliers provide a tight grip but may mar the metal findings in the process. If you're working with precious metals or doing a lot of metalwork, it's a good idea to use nonserrated pliers. | CRIMPING PLIERS | Crimping pliers have specialized grooved ends that work together to squeeze a crimping tube flat. If you're only flattening a crimp bead or a small crimp tube, you may be able to substitute a pair of needle-nose pliers. If you need to double crimp a standard crimp tube, there's no substitute for a pair of crimping pliers. It takes a little practice to get comfortable positioning the crimping tube in the appropriate grooves, but the resulting connection is very sturdy. | WIRE CUTTERS | Save your scissors by using wire cutters to trim all your wires and link chains. It's safer to make a quick clip with wire cutters than to exert too much pressure with scissors blades. | MEMORY WIRE CUTTERS (OPTIONAL) | Memory wire is strong and its coils withstand stretching when it's repeatedly pulled on and off the wrist, neck or finger. Memory wire cutters easily snip through this heavy-duty wire.

wire cutters

crimping pliers

scissors

Any good-quality scissors will work, but my scissors of choice are Fiskars Softouch Micro-Tip. They have small, sharp points that fit easily in tight places. The built-in spring is activated by a light touch on the handgrips. The center locking mechanism and plastic sleeve make them portable and easy to stow.

needles

I use size 12 beading needles in this book, but they come in lots of different sizes. Before you begin beading, verify that the beading thread passes easily through the eye of the needle and that the threaded needle passes easily through the smallest of the selected beads.

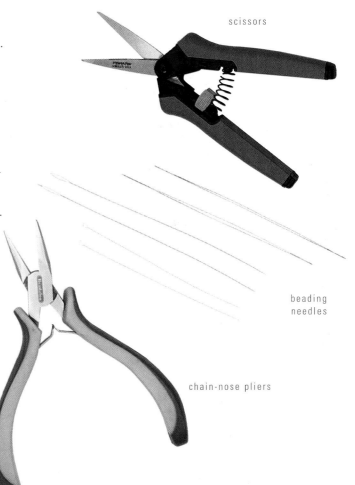

scissors

beading needles

chain-nose pliers

12

glues and adhesives

Ideally, beaded projects are stronger if they're strung, knotted or wired together. However, glue can come in handy. It can serve as a reinforcer to make a beaded element doubly secure, and it can be a time-saver, taking the place of knots. In the few cases in this book where glue is required, I've used G-S Hypo Cement.

| G-S HYPO CEMENT | This glue has a built-in applicator. To keep the applicator tip clear, a tiny wire threads in and out when the cap is screwed on or off. It's perfect for accurately inserting a drop of glue into tight spots or over small knots.

| TAPE | Keep clear tape with your beading supplies. A small piece wrapped around the end of the stringing wire will help prevent accidents and keep partially strung strands secure.

felt bead mats

storage container

storage containers

Plastic fishing tackle boxes are ideal for bead storage. Look for boxes with tight locking lids and sealed dividers that won't let beads slide out from under them. I use several boxes to organize my beads and sort them by variety (seed beads in one, glass beads sorted by color in another, stones and metal beads in a third). If you use a variety of beads and want to keep them separated, purchase an inexpensive sectioned china dish from a bead store. As your collection grows, continue to add boxes. Adjustable-divider tackle boxes are perfect for storing metal findings, threads, cords and wires.

work surface

Some people choose to purchase felted bead boards. I've found that stiff felt sheets sit better on my work surface and are easier to store. The texture helps prevent beads from rolling. Select a neutral gray or white sheet that doesn't hide the beads.

techniques

Despite the tremendous variety in finished beaded jewelry pieces, they all share the same basic techniques. Take a little time to familiarize yourself with these simple processes—especially how to shape head pins and how to secure clasps to the ends of beaded strands with crimp tubes. Once you're comfortable with the steps, you'll find assembling the actual projects very simple.

opening and closing a jump ring

Jump rings are handy connectors. You can use them to extend a finished piece before adding a clasp, or to join a short length of chain to one end. Thread a jump ring through a charm before stringing it onto the strand, and it will allow the charm to face the right way. The trick is to open and close jump rings laterally so they keep their shape.

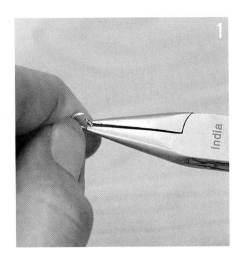

one • Hold one side of the jump ring between your thumb and index finger, just below the break in the metal. Grab the other side of the jump ring with your fingers or with chain-nose pliers and pull the wire toward you to open it. Be careful not to open the jump ring by pulling the wire ends away from each other, as horizontal action can distort the shape of the jump ring and weaken it.

two • Close the jump ring by sandwiching the wires between the pincers of the chain-nose pliers. Apply even pressure to bring the wire ends firmly back together.

linking eye pins

The straight end of an eye pin can be easily beaded and then bent to make a second loop. The loop ends can be connected to each other, to short lengths of chain or to clasps. Eye pins are very versatile, and incorporating them into your beaded jewelry gives you endless options. In fact, you can make an entire piece with linked beaded eye pins.

one • Hold the eye pin steady with your fingers and use round-nose pliers to open the eye pin loop.

two • Slide the eye pin loop onto the open loop. Use pliers to secure the opening closed again.

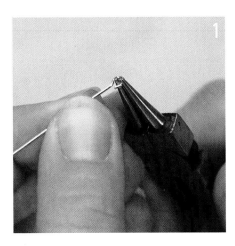

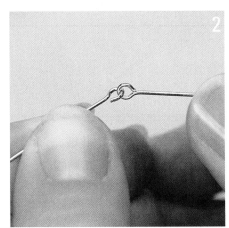

using crimp tubes

Use this double crimp technique when using no. 2 crimp tubes or larger. A single crimp will anchor the clasp to the strand but the second fold makes the connection even stronger. It also serves to narrow the crimp so it blends into the finished piece.

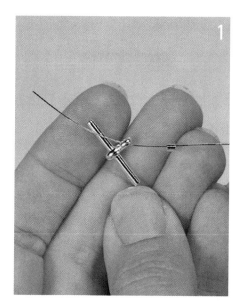

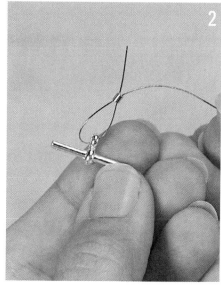

one · String one crimp tube followed by one part of the clasp onto the end of the strand. Position them about ½"–1" (1cm–3cm) from the end of the wire.

two · Fold the strand end back through the crimp tube. Pull the end to tighten the loop with the clasp.

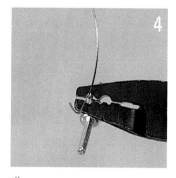

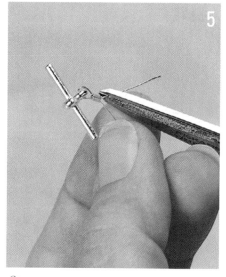

three · Separate the wires inside the crimp tube so they rest against opposite sides of the tube (wires should not cross inside the tube). Clamp the crimping pliers over the outside of the tube, aligning the bumps in the tool with the center of the tube. Squeeze the crimping tool to flatten the tube's center and simultaneously trap the strings on the sides.

four · Use one of the rounded openings in the crimping tool to bring the string sides of the tube together, essentially folding the flattened tube in half.

five · Separate the strands where they emerge from the crimp tube, and then carefully cut off the remaining wire end flush with the edge of the crimp tube.

turning a loop in a head pin

This technique transforms any bead into a charm or dangle. It is quick and easy to turn the wire end into a loop. The only drawback is that if the loop is pulled, it can come apart and fall off the jewelry. If you're placing the dangle where it might get caught or pulled, substitute the wrapped loop technique.

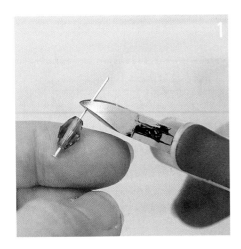

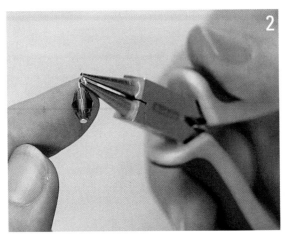

one · Slide a bead onto a head pin. Use wire cutters to cut the head pin wire to about ½" (13mm) above the bead. For larger beads, cut the wire to about ⅜" (1cm).

two · Grab the head pin wire near the end with round-nose pliers and twist them toward yourself to create a loop. Use round-nose and chain-nose pliers to make fine adjustments to secure the loop.

making a wrapped loop

A wrapped loop is the strongest way to finish a head pin and is the preferred way to make earrings. Don't skimp when buying head pins, especially when you're learning this technique. Sterling head pin wires are so flexible you can almost wrap them with your fingertips. Wait until you're comfortable before using decorative head pins. They're made of layered metals that make them harder to manipulate.

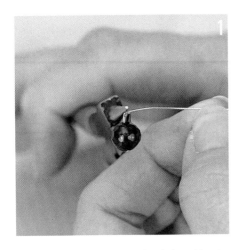

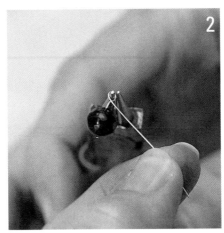

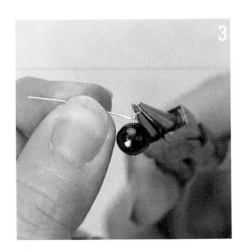

one · Slide a bead onto a head pin and bend the wire above the bead at a 90° angle with round-nose pliers.

two · Wrap the wire around the nose of the round-nose pliers to create a loop.

three · Hold the loop with the round-nose pliers and use your fingers or chain-nose pliers to wrap the tail end of the wire around the base of the loop several times. Trim away excess wire with wire cutters.

making a spiral wrap

This technique is a decorative extension of the wrapped loop. Stick with easy-to-wrap sterling head pins to ensure success. You'll be surprised how much sophistication this simple technique can add to even the plainest beaded dangle.

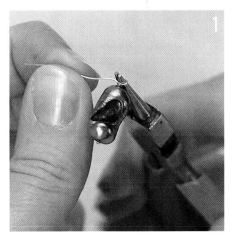
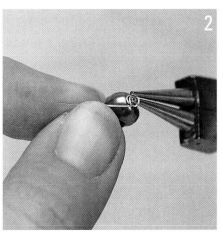

one • Slide a bead onto a head pin and bend the wire just above the bead at a 90° angle. Make a loop with the wire.

two • Begin to make a spiral with the wire using your fingers, wrapping the wire first around the base of the loop and working out from the center, over the top of the bead.

three • Continue to shape the wire with your fingers to create a spiral that covers the top of the bead. When the spiral is big enough, use wire cutters to trim off the excess tail.

linking earring components

Once head pins and jump rings have been beaded and shaped, it takes just seconds to hook them together into an earring. Once you've got the basic technique down, you can do endless variations on it. You may try looping several dangles onto a head pin loop or connect a chain of beaded head pins. Use your imagination—the possibilities are endless.

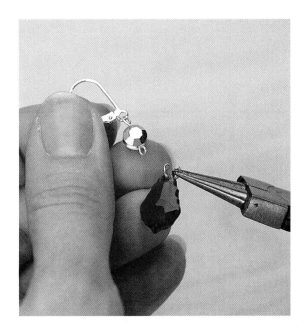

To begin, create the earring components. For example, to create the components for this earring, you'd slide a bead onto an eye pin and turn a loop above the bead, attaching it to the earwire. Then you'd slide another bead onto a jump ring. To construct the earring, simply slide the jump ring onto the bottom eye pin loop and close the jump ring using pliers.

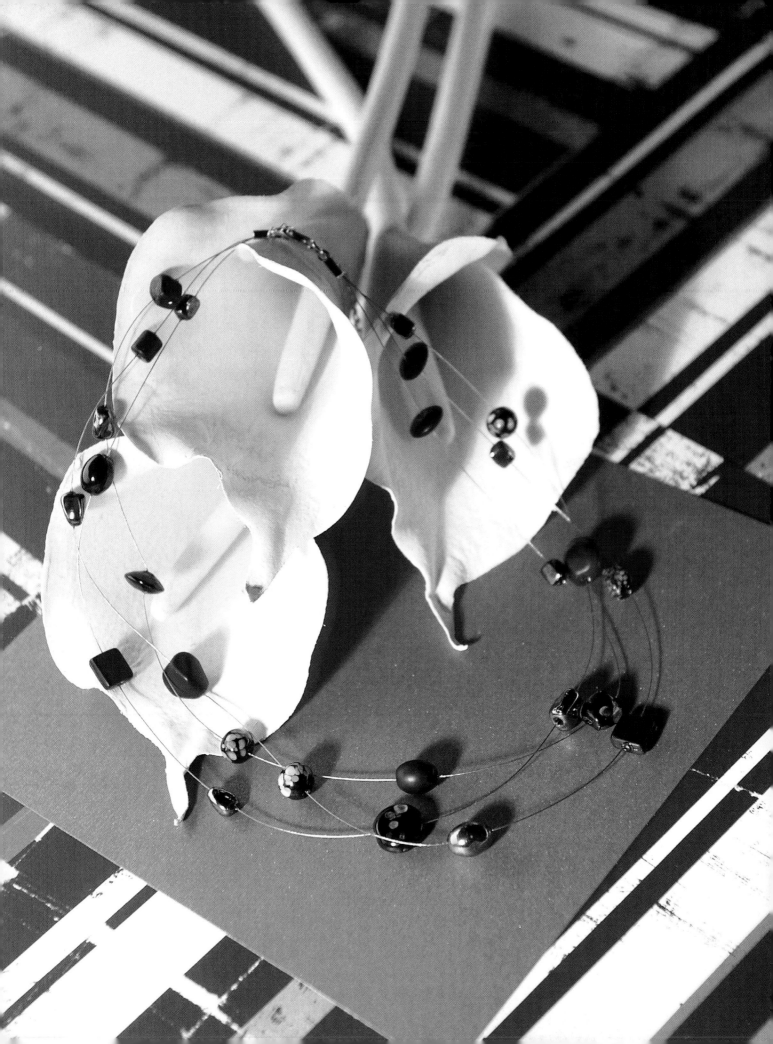

necklaces

There's no question that necklaces have become a vital part of today's fashion. Every time I switch on the news there's a broadcaster sporting a spectacular beaded necklace that sets off her jacket just so. Necklaces are the ideal accessory—they frame the face and draw attention to the neckline. A pearl or stone necklace can dress up a plain shirt, whereas a simply beaded long strand can make a dressy outfit more casual.

Beads are enjoying a veritable renaissance in popularity. They are being strung in so many different ways, and I believe they've become the focal point of decades of innovative jewelry design. Both the individual beads and fashion influences have inspired my beaded designs. It has been especially challenging to narrow down the wide array of choices to the following hand-picked selection of necklaces. I've included pieces that are bright and playful, like a sunny Summer Lariat perfect for summer and a colorful choker with butterfly dangles, as well as more classic and formal designs, like a string of vintage pearls and a necklace of cascading teardrops. Some designs can withstand everyday wear—such as the stone pendant—and others, like the glistening, delicate Beaded Chains—are for special evenings out.

Be sure you don't overlook the extra feature in this chapter—I've included matching earring designs to coordinate with many of the necklaces. Necklaces require larger quantities of beads than most other jewelry pieces, and I've often found that I have at least a couple of beads left over. Don't let them go to waste—it only takes a few minutes to assemble them into beautiful earrings that will complement your necklace.

CHAPTER

1

summer lariat

MATERIALS

Finished Length: 6'9" (2m),
including flowers

7' (2.1m) strand of .012 bright nylon-
coated stringing wire (Beadalon)

2 packages of Summer mini bead mix
(Blue Moon)

2 yellow blown glass flowers
(Blue Moon)

opaque yellow glass saucer beads

opaque yellow seed beads

2 no. 1 crimp beads

crimping pliers

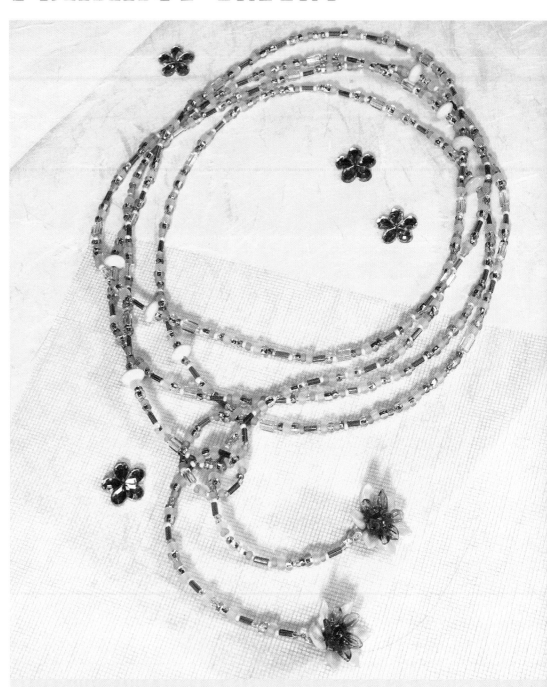

Brighten your day by wrapping this long stream of sunshine around your neck. Vibrant turquoise and orange beads contrast with the many shades of yellow and offset the cheerful glass flower beads on the ends of the lariat. There's no need for a clasp—just loop the flowered ends into a loose knot and make your own sunny day.

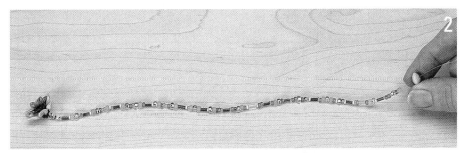

one · Attach a blown glass flower to one end of a 7' (2.1m) length of wire with a no. 1 crimp bead. Flatten the crimp bead with the crimping pliers to secure the flower.

two · String on 9" (23cm) of beads from the Summer mini bead mix along with opaque yellow seed beads in a random pattern. At the 9" (23cm) mark, string on an opaque yellow glass saucer bead. Continue stringing beads randomly onto the wire, stringing on a saucer bead at each 9" (23cm) interval.

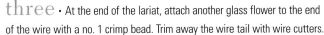

three · At the end of the lariat, attach another glass flower to the end of the wire with a no. 1 crimp bead. Trim away the wire tail with wire cutters.

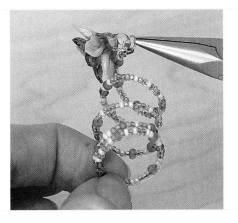

Cut four and a half coils of ring memory wire with wire cutters. Make a small loop at one end using round-nose pliers. String beads from the Summer mix onto the wire (skip the bugle beads) and make a small loop at the end with round-nose pliers to secure the beads. To finish the ring, attach a glass flower to the end loop with a 4 mm jump ring.

SUMMER RING

• ADD A TOUCH OF SUNSHINE to your fingertips with this coordinating ring.

The eye-catching blown glass flower is the perfect focal point for this simple ring.

See the accessories chapter for more memory wire rings (page 120).

pretty-in-pink choker

MATERIALS

Finished Length: 16" (41cm),
including clasp

19" (48cm) strand of .018 silver plated
stringing wire (Beadalon)

silver flower dangles (Blue Moon)

silver seed beads

pink *E* beads

pink Czech glass beads—flower beads,
flat oval, rectangle and small irregular
round beads

2 no. 1 crimp beads

filigree clasp (Blue Moon)

crimping pliers

wire cutters

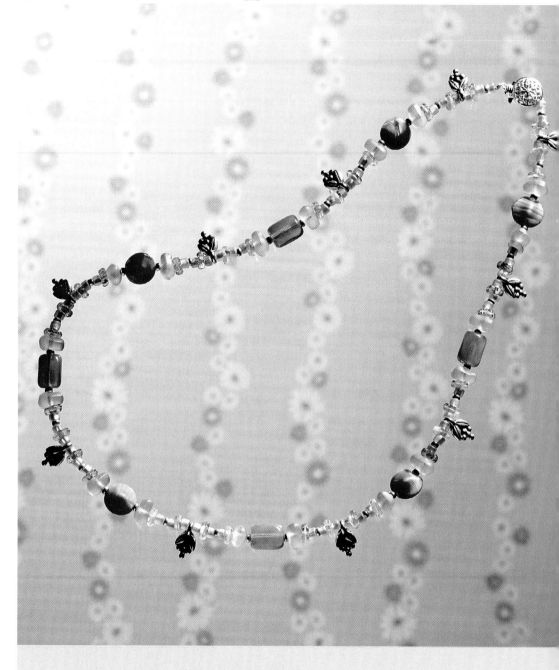

This very feminine necklace is strung with Czech glass beads in subtle shades of pink. The repeated pattern is punctuated by both silver seed beads and small flower dangles. If pink isn't your color of choice, simply choose strings of pressed glass beads in your favorite shade. If you need to increase the size of the dangles, select larger beads to match.

one • Attach a 19" (48cm) length of wire to one end of a filigree clasp with a crimp bead. String on the first segment of beads in the following pattern: *E* bead, silver seed bead, pink flower bead, *E* bead, silver flower dangle. Reverse pattern from the last *E* bead to the beginning of the pattern.

two • After completing the first segment of the pattern, continue stringing the beads in the following sequence: pink flower bead, irregular round pink bead, silver seed bead, flat pink oval bead, silver seed bead, irregular round pink bead, pink flower bead.

three • String the rest of the necklace by alternating between the two patterns, alternating between a flat oval bead and a rectangle bead in the second sequence. Attach the filigree end of the clasp to the end of the wire strand with a crimp bead. Flatten the crimp bead with the crimping pliers to finish.

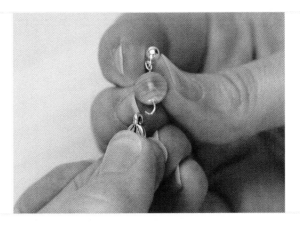

To make matching earrings, string a flat pink round bead onto an eye pin and link the loop end to an earwire. Cut the end of the eye pin wire and make a loop with round-nose pliers. Open the loop and slide on a silver flower dangle. Close the loop with pliers to finish the earring. Repeat for the other earring.

PRETTY-IN-PINK EARRINGS

• SILVER FLOWER DANGLES are perfect earring accents—use them to make instant earrings that need only a single round bead to set them off.

berry bead necklace

MATERIALS

Finished Length: 17" (43cm), including clasp

18" (46cm) strand of .018 bright nylon-coated stringing wire (Beadalon)

10mm Dazzle berry beads in three different coordinating colors (Westrim)

green- and silver-lined *E* beads

green seed beads

2 no. 2 gold crimp beads

hook and eye clasp (Darice)

crimping pliers

wire cutters

Who can resist these tantalizing berry beads? In the center of each bead is a plastic pearl bead that has been cleverly disguised with strands of dazzling seed beads. Available in a myriad of colors, pick your favorite and simply pair them with coordinating *E* and seed beads. An understated hook and eye clasp is the perfect finishing touch for this cheerful little necklace.

one • Cut a strand of stringing wire 18" (46cm) and attach the eye clasp to one end with a no. 2 gold crimp bead. String on a green-lined *E* bead, a silver-lined *E* bead, a seed bead, another silver-lined *E* bead, a green-lined *E* bead and a Dazzle berry bead. Continue stringing the beads in the established pattern until you have beaded about 16" (41cm).

two • Attach the hook end of the hook and eye clasp with a crimp bead to finish the necklace.

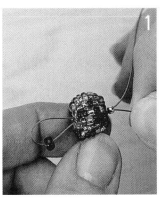

one • Cut a 38" (97cm) length of wire. Thread a gold crimp bead followed by a Dazzle berry bead onto one end of the wire, and then thread on a red *E* bead. Thread the wire back through the berry bead and through the crimp bead. Flatten the crimp bead with the crimping pliers to secure the bead.

two • Bead the length of the lariat randomly with beads from a red bead mix. Secure the berry bead by threading on a gold crimp bead, a berry bead and an *E* bead. Thread the wire back through the berry bead and back through the crimp bead. Flatten the crimp bead to secure. Trim off the excess wire tail with wire cutters.

BERRY LARIAT

• HAVE TWO BERRY BEADS LEFT OVER? Then make another necklace.

Simply crimp one to each end of a long beaded strand. No clasp necessary—just

bring the berry beads together and tie them into a loose overhand knot.

leather choker

MATERIALS

Finished Length: 17¾" (45cm),
including clasp

17½" (44cm) strand of leather cord

polished turquoise stone bead

decorative head pin (Blue Moon)

silver-plated tube-style cord ends
(Beadalon)

lobster clasp and 2" (5cm) strand of
chain (Beadalon)

2 4.5mm silver jump rings

G-S Hypo Cement

round-nose pliers

chain-nose pliers

This casual choker is perfectly suited for everyday wear. Take time to select your favorite polished stone to feature as the pendant. If you wear brown more often than black, switch the color of the leather cord to match your personal style.

one • To make the dangle, slide the turquoise stone onto a decorative head pin and create a wrapped loop at the top using round-nose pliers (see Techniques, page 16).

two • Apply a dab of G-S Hypo Cement to the inside of one of the silver-plated cord ends and adhere it to one end of the cord. Slide the pendant onto the open end of the leather cord.

three • Glue on the remaining silver-plated tube-style cord end with G-S Hypo Cement. Allow the glue to dry completely.

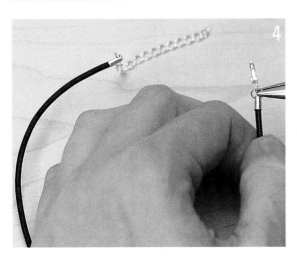

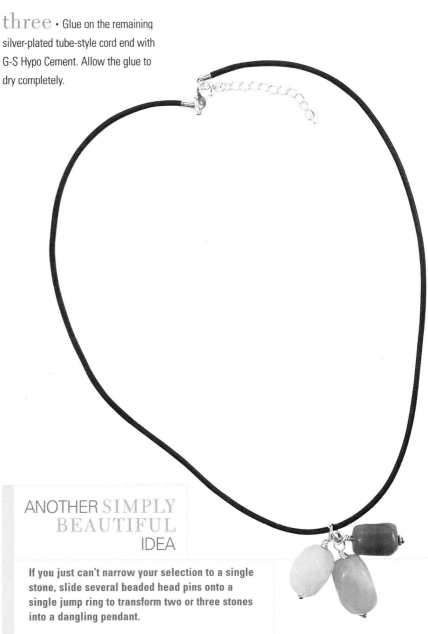

four • Attach a 2" (5cm) section of premade chain to one of the cord ends. Attach the lobster clasp to the remaining cord end. If necessary, use 4.5mm jump rings to connect both the chain and the clasp to the cord ends.

ANOTHER SIMPLY BEAUTIFUL IDEA

If you just can't narrow your selection to a single stone, slide several beaded head pins onto a single jump ring to transform two or three stones into a dangling pendant.

vintage pearls

MATERIALS

Finished Length: 16½" (42cm),
including clasp

6mm and 8mm smoke iridescent fire-
polished crystals (Darice)

6mm and 10mm ecru round glass pearls
(CCA Corp.)

2" (5cm) eye pins

ornate toggle clasp (Blue Moon)

round-nose pliers

chain-nose pliers

wire cutters

J ust like a necklace you might come across in your grand-
mother's jewelry box, this timeless strand of pearls will
never fall out of fashion. Individual pearls and fire-
polished crystals are threaded onto eye pins and then hooked
together to make a sturdy chain. This project is perfect for
recycling beads from broken necklaces. If you don't have
beads on hand, glass pearls are both readily available
and inexpensive.

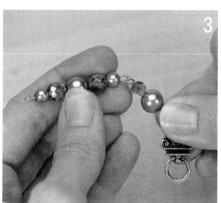

one • To create the first beaded component of the necklace, first open the eye pin loop with pliers. Link the eye pin to the circle end of the toggle clasp and close the loop again. Slide a 6mm smoke iridescent fire-polished crystal, a 10mm ecru pearl and another 6mm crystal onto the eye pin. Trim the wire to ⅜" (1cm) above the beads with wire cutters.

two • Use round-nose pliers to turn a loop at the top of the beads (see Techniques, page 16).

three • Create another beaded link with a 6mm pearl, 8mm crystal, 10mm pearl, 8mm crystal, 6mm pearl. Link that beaded eye pin to the first beaded component. Continue linking beaded components, alternating between the two patterns.

four • To finish the necklace, thread a 6mm crystal onto an eye pin and trim the wire to ⅜" (1cm) above the bead. Create a small loop above the bead with round-nose pliers and attach it to the final component in the necklace. Attach the other loop of this final beaded link to the bar end of the toggle clasp to finish.

ANOTHER SIMPLY BEAUTIFUL IDEA

The length of your pearl necklace is completely adjustable. You might consider linking additional beaded eye pins to the strand so it swings below your neckline. This classic variation skips the crystal beads and pairs two colors of pearls.

peridot drop lariat

MATERIALS

Finished Length: 19¼" (49cm)

26" (66cm) strand of .018 gold nylon-coated stringing wire (Beadalon)

peridot teardrop

4mm glass pearls (CCA Corp.)

1 each of 6mm and 10mm glass pearls (CCA Corp.)

6mm and 4mm clear crystals (Swarovski)

round peridot beads

freshwater pearls (Blue Moon)

gold wheel spacer beads (Blue Moon)

gold barrel spacer beads (Blue Moon)

gold and pearl seed beads

2 no. 1 gold-plated crimp beads (Beadalon)

crimping pliers

wire cutters

scissors

Peridot stones, sparkling crystals, subtle pearls and gold accent beads are strung together in a repeated pattern to create this elegant lariat. Fasten the lariat by dropping the teardrop peridot stone through the ring of gold seed beads, and adjust the necklace to fit the contour of your neck. If you're wearing an open-back dress, consider fastening the necklace at the back of the dress to create a bit of unexpected drama.

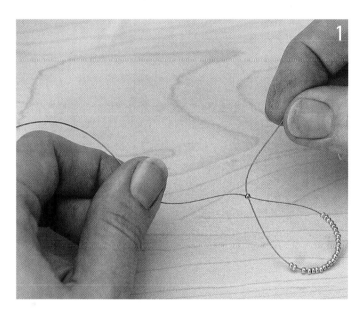

one • Cut a 26" (66cm) length of wire and thread on a gold crimp bead and 24 gold seed beads. Thread the end of the wire back through the crimp bead to make a loop. Flatten the crimp bead with the crimping pliers to secure the loop.

two • Thread the end of the wire through a gold spacer bead and a 6mm glass pearl and trim the wire tail with scissors or wire cutters.

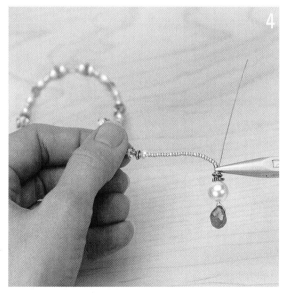

three • Begin to string the beads onto the wire in the following pattern: gold wheel spacer, 4mm pearl, gold seed bead, 4mm crystal, gold seed bead, 4mm pearl, gold wheel spacer, 4mm pearl, gold seed bead, pearl seed bead, gold seed bead, freshwater pearl, gold seed bead, peridot, gold seed bead, freshwater pearl, gold seed bead, pearl seed bead, gold seed bead, 4mm pearl, gold barrel spacer, 6mm crystal. Reverse the pattern beginning with a gold barrel spacer bead and ending with a 4mm pearl.

four • Continue to string beads onto the lariat in the established sequence until the beaded length measures about 17" (43cm). Then thread on 1¼" (3cm) of gold seed beads. To create the dangle at the end of the lariat, thread on a crimp bead, a gold wheel spacer, a gold barrel spacer, a 10mm pearl and a peridot teardrop. Thread the wire back up through the pearl, the spacers and the crimp bead. Flatten the crimp bead with the crimping pliers. Trim away the excess wire to finish.

floating beads necklace

MATERIALS

Finished Length: 18" (46cm),
including clasp

3 22" (56cm) long strands of .015 bright
nylon-coated stringing wire (Beadalon)

black glass bead mix (Darice)

lobster clasp (Blue Moon)

3½" (9cm) premade chain

1½" (4cm) silver head pin

2 crimp end connectors

4mm silver jump ring

G-S Hypo Cement

ruler

chain-nose pliers

round-nose pliers

crimping pliers

wire cutters

S urprisingly simple to assemble, this necklace is made
  by gluing the beads at intervals along the stringing
  wire. The only trick is waiting for the glue to dry before
grouping the strands together. This is an extremely versatile
technique, so feel free to experiment with different bead
varieties to create new effects. For instance, small pearls
will make delicate strands, whereas brightly colored miracle
beads will make a vibrant finished necklace.

one · Randomly string nine beads onto each of the three strands, arranging the beads so they're spaced 2½" (6cm) from the ends and 1½" (4cm) apart. Squeeze glue into each bead hole, then leave the beads undisturbed until the glue has completely dried, preferably overnight.

two · Hold the wires together at one end and secure them together with a crimp end connector, using the crimping pliers to fold each of the side flaps over the wires to trap them in place. Trim away the excess wires where they emerge from the connectors.

three · Attach a lobster clasp to one of the crimp end connectors using pliers to open the loop on the clasp. Slide the clasp onto the loop of the crimp end connector and use pliers to close the loop to secure the clasp.

four · Measure out 3½" (9cm) of premade chain and open one of the links to separate it. Attach the 3½" (9cm) length of chain to the free crimp end connector with a 4mm jump ring. Slide a small square black bead onto a head pin and create a loop at the top to attach it to the last link of the chain.

crystal garden necklace

MATERIALS

Finished Length: 15½" (39cm),
including clasp

2 36" (91cm) strands of 32-gauge
beading wire (Westrim)

4mm, 6.5mm, 8mm and 9mm
fire-polished crystals in assorted colors
including red, turquoise, topaz, pink,
fuchsia, teal and purple (Darice)

yellow, red, turquoise, purple, pearl,
light, dark and silver-lined
green seed beads

light, dark and silver-lined
green bugle beads

sterling toggle clasp (Darice)

wire cutters

tape

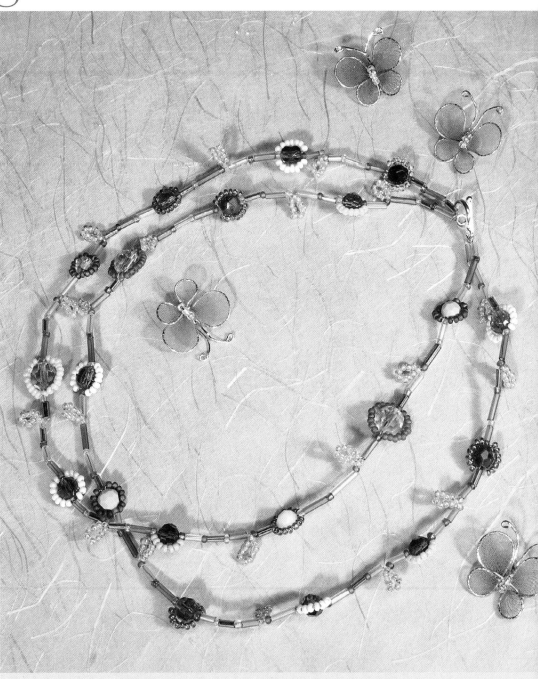

This miniature garland blooms all year round with unexpected brightly colored flowers. Each flower is simply made by looping seed bead petals around a crystal bead flower center. If you don't have time to make both strands, stop with just one or consider making a bracelet or even just a pair of single-stem leaf and flower earrings.

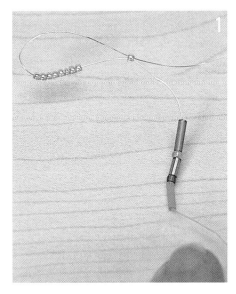 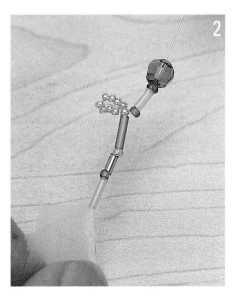 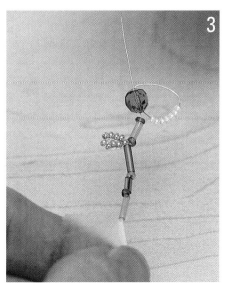

one · Before stringing the beads, tape one end of the wire with clear tape to hold the beads in place. Thread three bugle beads separated by seed beads onto the 32-gauge beading wire. Slide on nine seed beads and thread the wire back through the first seed bead to make the first leaf.

two · String on another bugle bead, a seed bead, and a 6.5mm crystal for the center of the first flower.

three · String seven seed beads onto the wire and thread it back through the crystal to create the "petals" on one side of the bead.

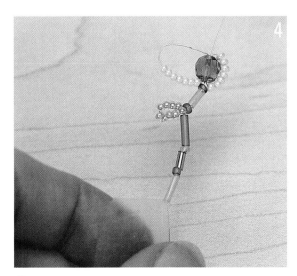 

four · String seven seed beads onto the wire and thread it back through the crystal again, this time forming the "petals" on the other side of the crystal flower center. Continue to string stems, leaves and crystal flowers. Use different sizes of crystals for the flower centers, each of which requires a different number of seed beads. For 4mm and 6.5mm crystals, string seven seed beads on each side. The 8mm beads require nine beads on each side, and 9mm crystals require ten beads on each side. End the first strand by alternating between three bugle beads and three seed beads. Bead the second strand in the same manner as the first, but don't include leaves at the beginning or end.

five · Attach each end of each beaded strand to either piece of the clasp by wrapping the end of the wire securely around the loops in each end of the clasp. Twist the wire tails around the ends of the strands in front of the clasp to secure the necklace. Trim the ends of the wire to finish.

butterfly dangle choker

MATERIALS

Finished Length: 15" (38cm), including clasp

20" (51cm) strand of .018 gold-plated stringing wire (Beadalon)

Summer Splash glass bead mix (Blue Moon)

6mm round turquoise beads (Swarovski)

red, turquoise, yellow and green seed beads

gold-plated head pins

gold lobster clasp and 2" (5cm) or pre-made chain (Beadalon)

0.8 gold-plated crimp beads (Beadalon)

round-nose pliers

crimping pliers

wire cutters

Perfect for the young at heart, this colorful necklace with its sweet glass heart, flower and butterfly beads is hard to resist. Transforming beads into charms is quick and easy—and it's a great way to create a consistent design. Next time you find an irresistible bead variety, consider using this technique to transform them into dangles.

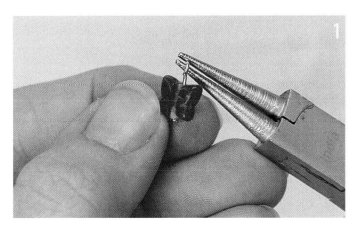

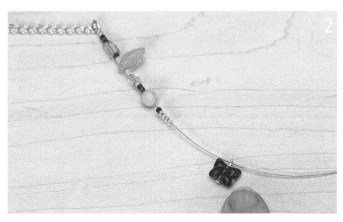

one · Begin making the necklace by making the dangles. Slide a butterfly bead onto a gold head pin and trim the wire to about ¼" (61mm) above the bead. Create a loop with the head pin wire using round-nose pliers and wrap the tail end of the wire around the base of the loop two times (see Techniques, page 16). Create more dangles using other kinds of beads—use flowers and hearts as well as butterflies.

two · Attach 2" (5cm) of premade gold chain to the wire with a crimp bead. String seed beads and other beads onto the wire in a random pattern for about ½" to 1½" (1cm to 4cm). Then string on a dangle and continue randomly stringing beads and dangles at the same intervals.

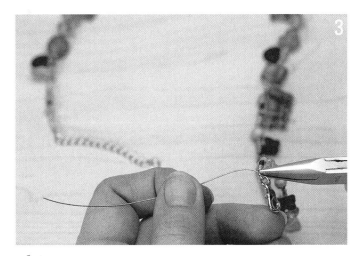

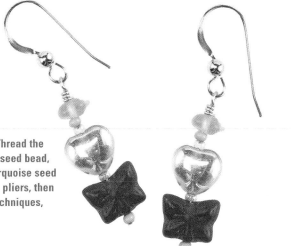

three · Finish stringing the beads and attach a gold lobster clasp to the end with a gold crimp bead, flattening it with the crimping pliers or chain-nose pliers to secure the clasp.

four · To create a dangle for the end of the chain, string another bead on a head pin and loop it around the last link in the chain. Fasten the necklace by hooking the lobster clasp to the desired length of chain link.

ANOTHER SIMPLY BEAUTIFUL IDEA

Use leftover beads to make playful matching heart and butterfly earrings. Thread the following bead sequence onto a 1¼" (3cm) gold-plated head pin: turquoise seed bead, red butterfly bead, green seed bead, blue heart bead, yellow seed bead, turquoise seed bead, yellow glass bead. Shape the end of the head pin around round-nose pliers, then thread the earwire onto the shaped wire before wrapping it closed (see Techniques, page 16).

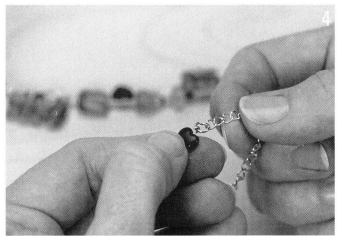

graduated indigo trio

MATERIALS

Finished Lengths, not including clasp:

top strand: 14½" (37cm)

middle strand: 17" (43cm)

bottom strand: 22½" (57cm)

17" (43cm), 20" (51cm) and 24" (61cm) strands of .013 bright nylon-coated stringing wire (Beadalon)

turquoise and purple flat AB glass bead mix (CCA Corp.)

dark amethyst luster and purple luster seed beads

6 no. 1 silver crimp tubes

three-strand silver hook and eye clasp

crimping pliers

wire cutters

tape

ruler

Slip on this swinging three-strand necklace and you might just feel like dancing to set it in motion. For anyone who loves the blues, this monochromatic necklace gets a shimmer of added color from the AB, or aurora borealis (oil slick), coated glass beads. Fire-polished crystal beads are a good substitute if you're unable to find the coated glass beads.

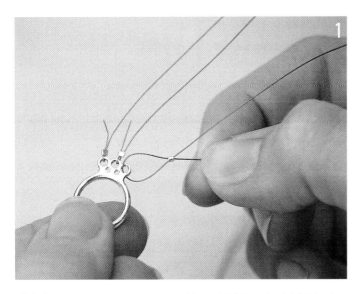

one · Cut three strands of wire to 17" (43cm), 20" (51cm) and 24" (61cm). Attach each length of wire to one of the loops on one end of the clasp with no. 1 crimp tubes using the crimping pliers to flatten them closed. Trim away the wire tails with wire cutters.

two · Begin with one of the wires and string on about ½" to 2½" (1cm to 6cm) of seed beads between stringing on glass beads. Position the smaller glass beads at the beginning and end of each strand where they're less likely to irritate your neck. Save the bigger beads for the center of the necklace where they'll be noticed.

three · Finish stringing the glass and seed beads for each of the three wires. Space the glass beads on each strand so they are staggered with the glass beads on the other strands. You will end up with 14½" (37cm), 17" (43cm) and 22½" (57cm) of beading, respectively. As you finish one strand, secure the end with a piece of tape so the beads don't fall off.

four · Attach the free end of each wire strand to each loop on the other end of the clasp with no. 1 crimp tubes. Flatten each crimp tube with the crimping pliers. Trim off the ends of each strand flush to the crimp tubes with wire cutters.

faceted stone pendant necklace

MATERIALS

Finished Length: 19" (48cm), including clasp

2 20" (51cm) strands of .018 bright nylon-coated stringing wire (Beadalon)

12" (30cm) strand of 26-gauge sterling wire (Darice)

carved stone (Blue Moon)

freshwater pearl (Blue Moon)

adventurine chips (Blue Moon)

pearl seed beads

2 no. 2 crimp tubes

sterling filigree clasp (Darice)

round-nose pliers

chain-nose pliers

crimping pliers

wire cutters

An intriguing mixture of stone finishes and bead scale make this necklace particularly eye-catching. The rough edges of the stone chips contrast pleasingly with the smooth seed beads and faceted stone pendant. The limited color palette of adventurine paired with the natural shade of the pearls brings the elements together to make a classic piece equally suited for business or casual wear.

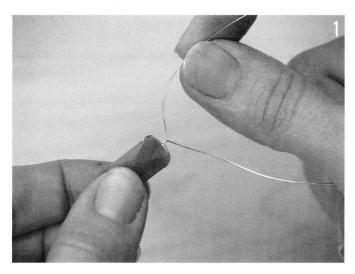

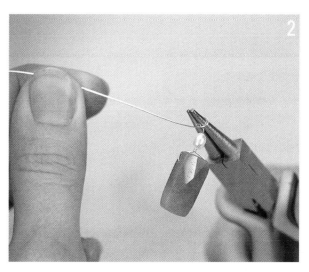

one · Begin making the stone pendant by stringing a 12" (30cm) length of 26-gauge wire through the hole in the faceted stone. Then twist the short end around the longer end two times. Cut off the shorter of the two wire tails with wire cutters.

two · String a pearl onto the remaining wire. Create a loop in the wire with round-nose pliers and wrap the end of the wire twice around the base of the loop. Trim off the excess wire with wire cutters.

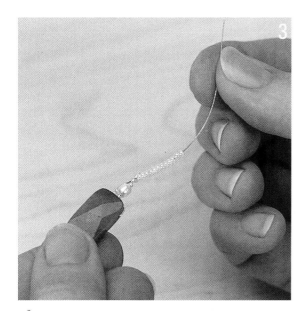

three · String a 20" (51cm) length of wire with pearl seed beads (18" [46cm] total length of beading). Slide the pendant onto the pearl strand.

four · String the remaining length of wire with 17¾" (45cm) of adventurine chips. Attach both wires to the clasp with a single crimp tube and flatten it awith crimping pliers. Crimp the tube a second time to fold it in half (see Techniques, page 15). Repeat on the other end of the wires to secure the other side of the clasp.

double-strand memory wire choker

MATERIALS

2 lengths of necklace-size memory wire cut to encircle your neck (Beadalon)

4.5mm brown fire-polished crystals (Darice)

2 two-hole spacers

14mm x 16mm rectangle topaz blue with foil bead (Blue Moon)

blue and gold Japanese seed beads

decorative silver-plated head pin (Blue Moon)

round-nose pliers

chain-nose pliers

wire cutters

G-S Hypo Cement

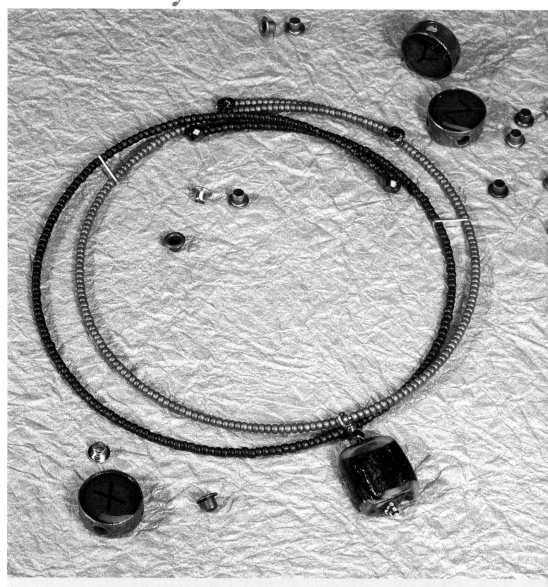

I n this case, two coils of wire are better than one—especially when they're cleverly connected with spacer bars. The wires are strung with blue and gold seed beads to complement the colors in the foil glass bead pendant. Clasps are unnecessary because the tension of the memory wire holds the choker in place and allows the wire to adjust to any size neck.

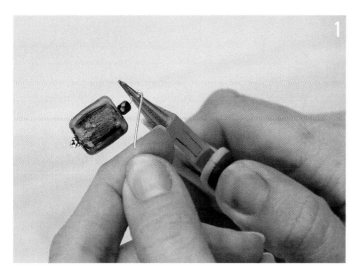

one • Thread a rectangle topaz blue with foil bead and a fire-polished crystal onto a decorative silver-plated head pin. Use round-nose pliers to create a loop at the top of the beads. Wrap the wire tail around the base of the loop and trim off the excess wire with wire cutters (see Techniques, page 16).

two • Cut two separate curls of necklace-size memory wire of exactly the same length using wire cutters. Glue a fire-polished crystal onto one end of each wire with G-S Hypo Cement. Allow the glue to dry completely, preferably overnight.

three • Thread one quarter of the length of one of the memory wire strands with blue Japanese seed beads. Slide on one two-hole spacer. Thread one half of the memory wire strand with more blue seed beads. Slide on the other two-hole spacer.

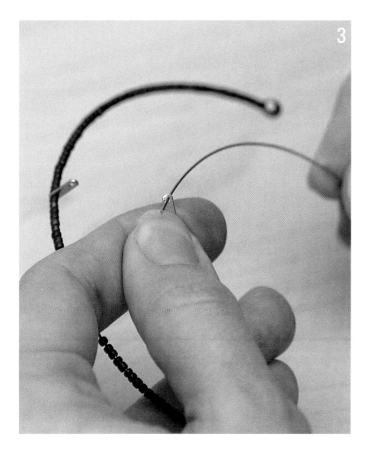

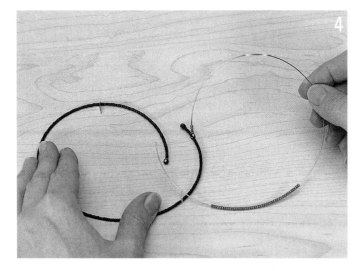

four · Finish beading the remaining quarter of the memory wire. Glue a fire-polished crystal onto the end of the memory wire to secure the beaded wire. Allow the glue to dry completely. Bead the first quarter of the second strand of memory wire with gold seed beads. Thread the memory wire through the free hole in one of the spacers.

gluing tip

The only hitch in assembling this choker is waiting for the glue to dry between beading sections of the memory wire. If you move a fire-polished bead while the glue is drying, you risk having the seed beads fall off the wire. Set up this project in an area where it can be left undisturbed while the glue dries. If you just can't wait, consider turning the ends over with chain-nose pliers (see Linked Memory Wire Cuff, page 80).

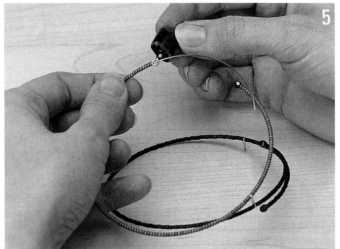

five · Continue to bead another half of the memory wire strand with gold seed beads. Thread the pendant onto the strand of gold seed beads.

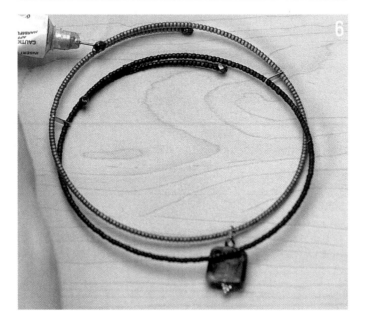

six · Thread the free end of the strand through the second two-hole spacer. Bead the final quarter of the memory wire with gold seed beads and glue on another fire-polished crystal to finish. Let the necklace dry in the open air, without moving it overnight, or until the glue dries.

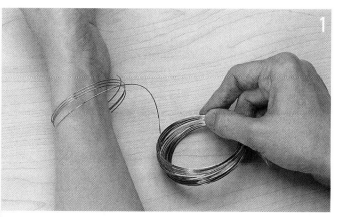

MEMORY WIRE BRACELET

- **THIS BEAUTIFUL MATCHING BRACELET IS THE PERFECT SHOWCASE** for additional foil glass beads. Silver spacers frame each glass bead and coordinate the finished bracelet with silver jewelry. A cinch to bead, the bracelet simply coils around the wrist automatically, adjusting to any size.

one • Coil bracelet-size memory wire four times around your wrist. Cut the length of wire with wire cutters.

two • Glue a fire-polished crystal onto the end of the wire with G-S Hypo Cement. Let it dry completely. Thread gold seed beads onto one third of the first coil. String on a 4mm fire-polished crystal, a silver spacer, a round topaz blue foil bead, a silver spacer and another 4mm fire-polished crystal. Bead another third of a coil with seed beads, and thread on a fire-polished crystal.

three • Continue to bead the entire bracelet, alternating between seed beads, the foil bead sequence and a single fire-polished crystal. Glue on a final fire-polished crystal to finish the bracelet. Allow the bracelet to air dry overnight or until the glue dries completely.

wired pearls necklace

MATERIALS

Finished Length: 15¼" (39cm), including clasp

rice pink freshwater pearls (Blue Moon)

1½" (4cm) sterling silver head pins

spring clasp

round-nose pliers

wire cutters

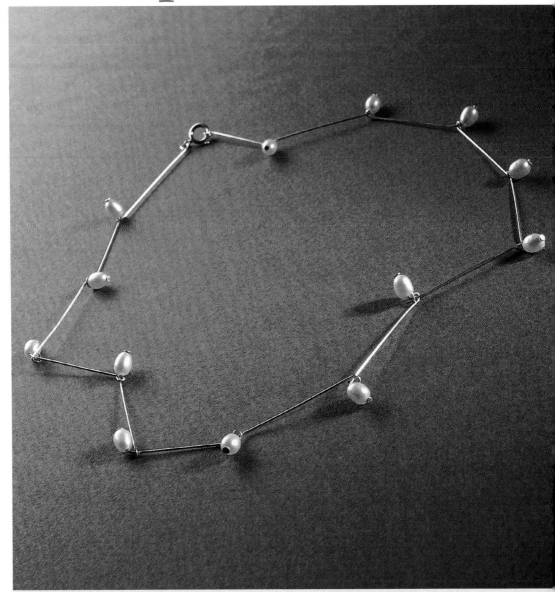

S himmering rice pink pearls are threaded onto individual sterling silver head pins to create this beautiful choker. The beaded head pins are simply linked together to form a lightweight elongated chain. This delicate necklace shows best when worn with an open neckline.

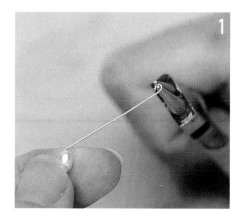

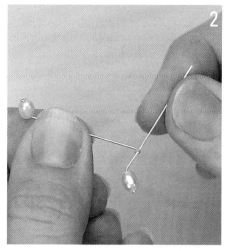

one • Slide a rice pink freshwater pearl onto a head pin and bend the wire up at about a 45° angle. Use round-nose pliers to create a loop at the open end.

two • Slide another freshwater pearl onto another head pin and bend the wire up as you did in step one. Slide the open end of the head pin through the loop on the first head pin and slide it up so the pearl rests at the loop. Create a loop at the open end of the head pin with round-nose pliers. Continue connecting pearls on head pins a total of 13 times.

storing tip > The unique construction makes this necklace especially vulnerable to breaking or bending. Store it flat or hang it alone, and be careful not to inadvertently bend the wires.

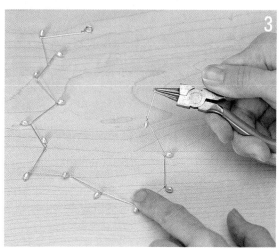

three • Coil the very end of the last head pin tightly around the very end of the round-nose pliers two times to create a double loop that will be part of the clasp. Also link a spring clasp to the loop in the first head pin.

To make the earrings, first create the pearl dangles. Slide three freshwater pearls onto three head pins and cut the wires above the beads at graduated lengths. Then use round-nose pliers to turn a loop at the top of each head pin wire. Simply link each of the dangles to the loop on the earwires to finish.

PEARL DANGLE EARRINGS

• **THESE EARRINGS WILL ATTRACT ATTENTION** even when worn without the matching necklace. The individual head pins allow the pearls to swing freely with every turn of your head.

cascading teardrops necklace

MATERIALS

Finished Length: 16" (41cm), including clasp

2 20" (51cm) strands of .006 black Dandyline stringing thread (Beadalon)

silver-lined purple seed beads

purple *E* beads

amethyst glass dagger beads

purple Japanese seed beads

silver end cups

spring ring and tag clasp

G-S Hypo Cement

beading needle

wire cutters

tape

crimping pliers

Strung on beading thread, this attractive lacework of purple glass beads drapes beautifully around the neckline. The elongated glass teardrop beads add dimension to the narrow strands of *E* and seed beads. Teardrop beads come in a range of colors, shapes and lengths. You can substitute almost any variety—just be sure you coordinate your selection with the color of the *E* and seed beads.

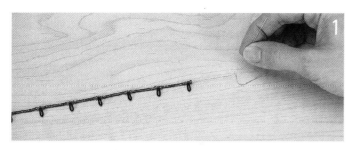

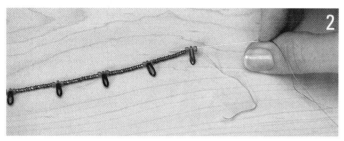

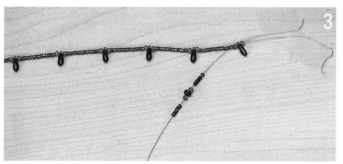

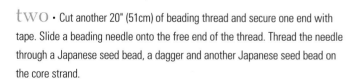

one · Cut a 20" (51cm) strand of beading thread and fold a piece of tape around one end. Slide a beading needle onto the free end. Thread beads onto the thread (the core strand) in the following sequence: Japanese seed bead, dagger bead, Japanese seed bead, 15 silver-lined purple beads. Continue stringing beads in this sequence until you reach a beaded length of about 15¾" (40cm). Tape the other end of the thread.

two · Cut another 20" (51cm) of beading thread and secure one end with tape. Slide a beading needle onto the free end of the thread. Thread the needle through a Japanese seed bead, a dagger and another Japanese seed bead on the core strand.

three · String on six purple Japanese seed beads, a silver-lined purple seed bead, a purple *E* bead, another silver-lined bead and six more purple Japanese seed beads.

four · Thread the needle through the next sequence of Japanese seed bead, dagger, seed bead on the core strand. Continue threading the needle through the core strand beads and stringing the sequence of beads onto the secondary strand 16 more times.

five · Thread both strands at both ends of the necklace through end cups and then tie the two ends together inside the end cup. Apply a dab of G-S Hypo Cement to secure the knots.

six · Slide the tag onto the end cup hook and crimp the hook closed using the crimping pliers. Repeat with the spring ring clasp on the other end of the necklace to finish.

crimped crystals necklace

MATERIALS

Finished Length: 27" (69cm),
including clasp

3 28" (71cm) strands of .018 gold-plated
nylon-coated beading wire (Beadalon)

no. 4 gold-plated crimp tubes

Sheer Elegance faceted coin mix with
amber AB and peridot AB beads
(CCA Corp.)

9mm x 6mm topaz and crystal beads
(Swarovski)

6mm and 5mm topaz and crystal beads
(Swarovski)

gold-plated tube-style magnetic clasp
(Beadalon)

crimping pliers

wire cutters

ruler

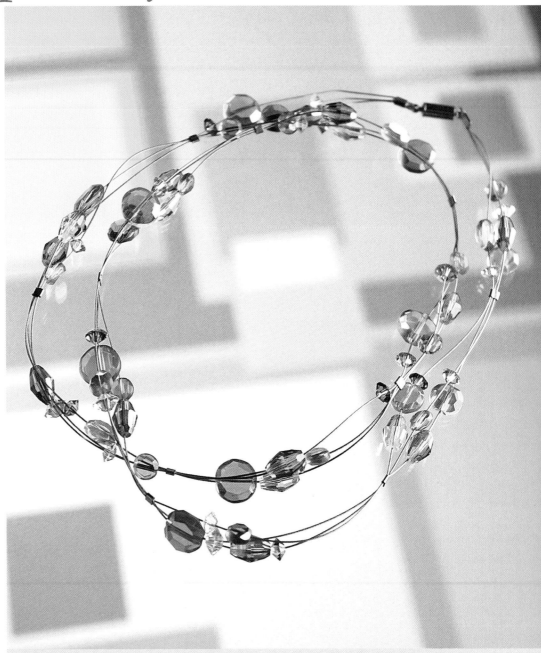

N othing is more alluring than a handful of sparkling crystals. In this necklace, crystals are clustered into enticing small groupings. The eye-catching variations in the shape, size, color and finish of each crystal bead cluster make this necklace appealing. The beads shine on golden stringing wires and are held in place by gold crimp tubes.

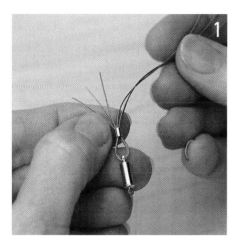

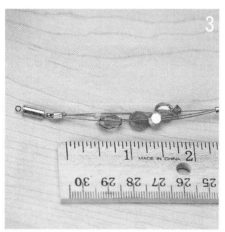

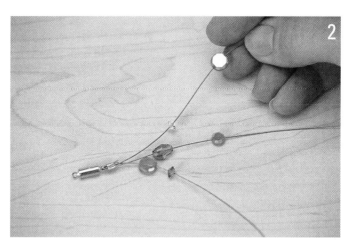

one · Cut three 28" (71cm) strands of .018 gold-plated wire and attach them to one end of a gold-plated tube-style magnetic clasp with a gold-plated crimp tube. Flatten the crimp tube with crimping pliers to secure the wires. Trim off the excess wire tails with wire cutters.

two · Randomly string two beads onto each wire (choose both crystal beads and beads from the coin mix).

three · To secure the first crimp station, measure 2½" (6cm) from the clasp and slide all three wires through a no. 4 crimp tube. Flatten the crimp tube with the crimping pliers.

*crystal tip > Try to distribute the different bead varieties between all of the groupings. You may want to arrange the bead groupings before you start stringing so you can make sure you have an attractive pattern. Also avoid placing two of the same kind of bead on the same wire within a single grouping.

four · Continue to string on beads and secure crimp tubes at 2½" (6cm) intervals. Secure ten more groupings of crystals to complete the necklace.

five · To finish the necklace, thread all three strands through a crimp tube, through the clasp and back through the crimp tube. Flatten the crimp tube to secure the clasp. Trim away any excess wire.

beaded chains

MATERIALS

Finished Length: 18" (46cm)

2 fine sterling silver link chains (CCA Corp.)

26-gauge silver wire (Darice)

light topaz and yellow 4mm crystal AB cubes (Swarovski)

jonquil AB 6mm bicones (Swarovski)

spring ring and tag clasp

2 4mm silver jump rings

round-nose pliers

chain-nose pliers

wire cutters

ruler

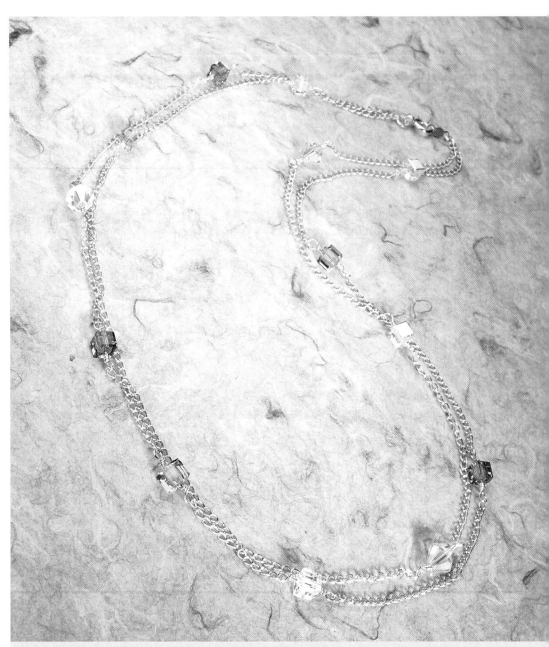

This delicate twinkling necklace is perfect for special occasions. Its elegant drape is the perfect complement to evening wear, adding just the right amount of glitz. Each crystal bead is suspended on a length of sterling wire between short pieces of lightweight chain. The understated fine chain lets the sparkling crystals take center stage.

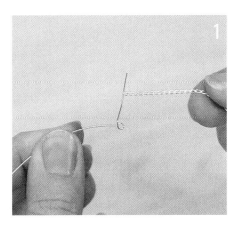

one · To create the first section of the necklace, measure out and separate a 1" (3cm) section of premade chain. Cut a 4" (10cm) length of 26-gauge wire and make a loop in the wire. Thread the wire through the link at one end of the chain section and allow the chain to settle in the loop.

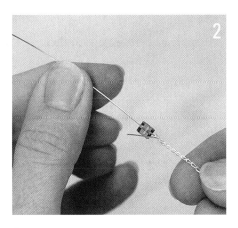

two · Slide a 4mm crystal onto the 26-gauge wire. Wrap the tail end of the wire around the base of the loop two times. Trim the excess wire tail with wire cutters.

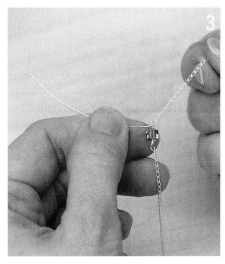

three · Link a 2" (5cm) section of premade chain to the other end of the wire by creating another wrapped loop.

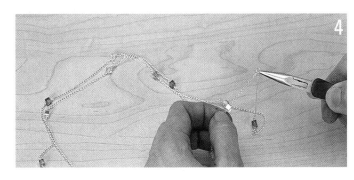

four · Continue to link 2" (5cm) sections of chain together with crystal cubes by creating wrapped loops in the following pattern: yellow cube, topaz cube, crystal cube, topaz cube, yellow cube, crystal cube. Finish the first chain with a 1" (3cm) section of chain. Repeat for the second chain in the following pattern with 2" (5cm) intervals of chain: jonquil bicone, crystal cube, jonquil bicone, yellow cube, jonquil bicone, topaz cube. Attach a 4mm jump ring to the end of one chain and link the other chain to that jump ring as well.

five · Finish the necklace by attaching the jump rings to the spring clasp.

CHAIN EARRINGS

· THESE SWINGING EARRINGS ARE SO LIGHTWEIGHT you might just forget you're wearing them. Those around you won't be likely to overlook them, though, when every time you turn your head the crystal beads reflect light and sparkle.

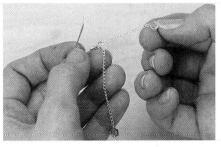

Use pliers to laterally open the base of the earwire. Hook a 3" (8cm) piece of leftover chain onto the earwire 1¼" (3cm) from one end and 1¾" (4cm) from the other end. Use ½" (1cm) head pins to attach a crystal cube to the longer end of the chain and a topaz cube to the shorter end.

silver flowers necklace

MATERIALS

FInished Length: 16" (41cm),
including clasp

3 19" (48cm) strands of .015 bright
nylon-coated stringing wire

silver twist beads

silver *E* and seed beads

metal flower beads (Darice)

metal flower spacers (Darice)

2" (5cm) silver-plated eye pins

6 no. 1 silver crimp beads

diamond toggle clasp (Blue Moon)

2 3.5mm jump rings

round-nose pliers

crimping pliers

wire cutters

tape

With shades of silver ranging from light to dark, the monochromatic color scheme in this necklace highlights the subtle tonal variations in all of the different beads used. The contrast in metal finishes from bright to muted also helps to create interest between the four necklace strands. Three of the strands are simply beaded onto stringing wire, and the fourth is made of metal flower spacers connected with beaded eye pins.

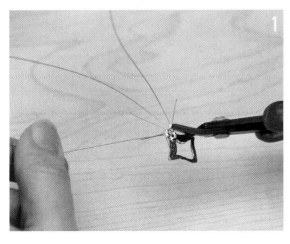

one · Attach three 19" (48cm) strands of wire to the diamond toggle clasp with crimp beads, using a separate crimp bead for each strand.

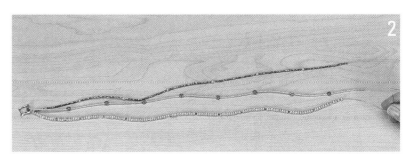

two · String each strand of wire in the following sequences: Strand one: ten silver *E* beads, one flower bead (repeat 13 times); Strand two: 30 seed beads, one flower bead (repeat eight times); Strand three: 25 silver twist beads, one silver *E* bead (repeat six times). Place a piece of tape at the end of each strand to secure the beads. Use three more crimp beads to connect the finished strands to the toggle end of the clasp.

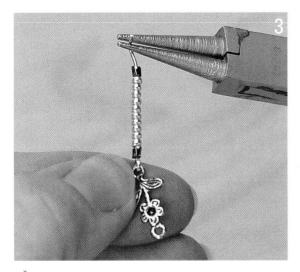

three · To make the final strand, first connect one end of an eye pin to a flower spacer. Then thread a twist bead, ten seed beads and another twist bead onto the eye pin. Make a loop on the other end of the eye pin with round-nose pliers.

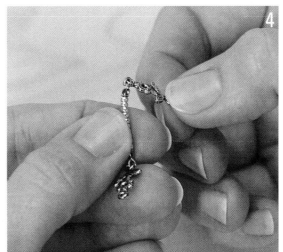

four · Connect another flower spacer to the new eye pin loop. (Repeat 11 times.)

sequencing tip > Don't hesitate to substitute different varieties of silver beads or create your own bead sequence. Just remember to make sure all the strands are the same length before attaching them to the second half of the clasp.

five · Use a jump ring to connect each end of the flower spacer strand to the clasp to finish the necklace.

bracelets

A flash of colorful beads around your wrist brightens your day and dresses up any outfit, even a well-worn pair of jeans. Whenever you reach for your keys or purse, the quick sparkle of your bracelet offers a pleasant distraction from the task at hand. Bracelets are perfect for my on-the-go life—I usually snap one around my wrist before running out the door.

Choose beaded bracelets that best suit your personal style so you have a selection to choose from each day. The understated elegance of the Chained Pearls and the Stone, Glass and Pearl Thirds bracelets are ideal for the workplace. The tiny, swinging crystals in the bracelet strung with flat pearls and the bright crystals in the Sparkle Bicone Bracelet will shimmer around your wrist, making them the perfect accompaniment to formal wear for evenings out on the town. If you're looking to add a little whimsy to your everyday style, try the unique Copper Tones Bracelet or the playful bracelet made of wired beads and fastened with a heart clasp.

If you have beads on hand, select a project that will best utilize your stash. For instance, single-strand bracelets like the Button Clasp Bracelet use smaller quantities of different bead varieties, whereas the multistrand Yellow Turquoise Bracelet requires five lengths of identical beads. Always save your leftover beads, and when looking over the projects in this book, you'll discover matching earring designs that complement the bracelets.

button clasp bracelet

MATERIALS

Finished Length: 6½" (17cm),
including clasp

12" (30cm) strand of .013 bright nylon-
coated stringing wire (Beadalon)

soapstone bead mix (Blue Moon)

ochre *E* beads

18mm x 13mm turquoise bead

assorted glass beads

silver spacer beads (Blue Moon)

silver bead caps (Blue Moon)

silver frame bead

¾" (2cm) wide silver button

2 no. 2 crimp tubes

crimping pliers

wire cutters

You don't always need traditional jewelry clasps on hand when you're beading. Look through a button jar to find the perfect clasp for this bracelet—after all, buttons are as varied and interesting as beads and clasps. And they're often one-of-a-kind, especially the vintage variety. If you prefer gold buttons, simply switch to gold stringing wire and gold-finished crimps, spacers and frame beads.

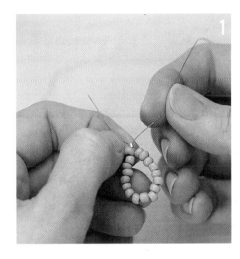

two · String on a random pattern of beads, using bead caps to accent bigger beads.

one · To create the beaded loop that will be the clasp, string about ¾" (2cm) of E beads onto a 12" (30cm) length of wire and form a loop by putting both ends of the wire through a crimp tube and flattening it to secure the loop. Make sure the loop is big enough to accommodate the button you are using for the clasp. Test the loop size before crimping.

three · Continue to string beads, occasionally accenting one bead with a silver frame bead, until you have 6½" (17cm) of beading.

four · Attach the button to the end of the wire with a crimp tube and use the crimping pliers to flatten it. Trim away the excess tail with wire cutters.

ANOTHER SIMPLY BEAUTIFUL IDEA

This subtle version of the bracelet showcases neutral colored beads in shades of tan, green and brown.

copper tones bracelet

MATERIALS

Finished Length: 7½" (19cm), including clasp

22" (56cm) strand of .015 gold-plated nylon-covered stringing wire (Beadalon)

8mm Erinite (grey/green) crystal beads (Swarovski)

6mm and 22mm x 8mm grey/blue freshwater pearls

bronze rice pearls

3 7mm round and one carved light blue-green teardrop fluorite stones

light green seed beads

bronze metal saucer bead

copper metal eye tube beads (Blue Moon)

4mm copper metal rounds with flowers (Blue Moon)

1 14mm copper metal flat round bead with flowers (Blue Moon)

2 11mm copper metal flat round beads with spiral (Blue Moon)

2 copper metal decorative head pins (Blue Moon)

copper metal toggle clasp (Blue Moon)

2 black crimp beads

crimping pliers

round-nose pliers

chain-nose pliers

Copper clasp, beads and head pins set this bracelet apart from more common silver and gold metal finishes. The blue-grey and green shades of freshwater pearls, polished fluorite stone beads and crystals contrast perfectly with the copper jewelry findings. Additional visual interest comes from the way the beading switches from single to double strand, both wires alternating between threading through the same series of beads and then separating to individually strung beads.

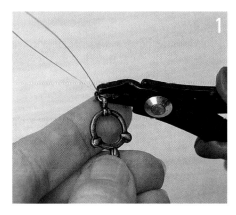

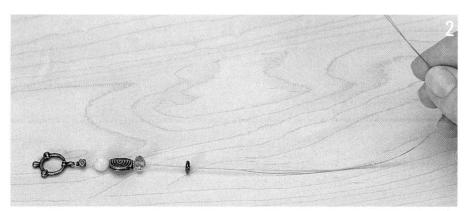

one · Thread the stringing wire through the clasp and bring both ends together so the clasp slides down to the center of the stringing wire. Thread both ends through a crimp bead and slide the bead down the wires so it rests against the clasp. Flatten the crimp bead with crimping pliers to secure the clasp.

two · String both wires through a 7mm round, a flat spiral, a crystal and a bronze saucer bead (or any combination of beads you like) until you reach about 1¼" (3cm).

three · Separate the wires and string about 1½" (4cm) of beads in a random pattern onto each one.

four · Create dangles by threading random beads onto decorative head pins. Trim the wire above the beads and turn loops at the top (see Techniques, page 16). Slide the dangles onto the stringing wire at random intervals. Continue to string beads, alternating between stringing beads onto both strands and separating the strands and beading them individually. To construct a bracelet like this one, bead 1¼" (3cm) with the strands together, ⅜" (1cm) apart, 1½" (4cm) together, ⅜" (1cm) apart and 1¼" (3cm) together.

five · To finish the bracelet, thread both strands through a crimp bead, through the loop on the bar end of the toggle clasp and back through the crimp bead. Flatten the crimp bead with the crimping pliers to secure the clasp. Trim away the excess wire tails to finish.

sparkle bicone bracelet

MATERIALS

Finished Length: 7½" (19cm), including clasp

2 18" (46cm) strands of .013 bright nylon-coated stringing wire (Beadalon)

6mm jonquil AB bicone crystals (Swarovski)

4mm peridot bicone crystals (Swarovski)

silver seed beads

round toggle set with AB rhinestones (Pure Allure Inc.)

2 no. 1 crimp beads

crimping pliers

With its shimmery green and yellow crystals punctuated by dots of silver seed beads, this bracelet is the epitome of glittering costume jewelry. The web of sparkling crystals is made with two separate beading strands. A square loop is formed when both strands thread through the same crystal and then separate and come together again to form a faceted lattice of crystals. Look for an ornate rhinestone-studded clasp to provide continuous sparkle from one end of the bracelet to the other.

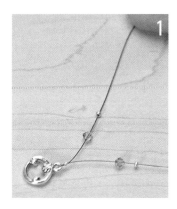

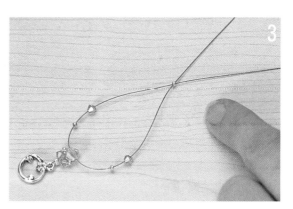

one · Slide the circle end of a toggle clasp onto an 18" (46cm) length of wire and fold the wire in half so that the clasp settles in the fold. Slide both ends of the wire through a crimp bead and flatten it to secure it. Separate the two strands of wire and thread one 4mm peridot crystal and one silver seed bead onto each strand.

two · Thread both strands in opposite directions through a 6mm jonquil crystal. Thread a silver seed bead onto each strand.

three · Thread a 4mm peridot crystal onto each strand. Thread both strands through a silver seed bead. Separate the strands and begin the pattern again.

four · Continue beading until you reach a total beaded length of about 7" (18cm). Attach the clasp to the other end using a crimp bead.

PURPLE SPARKLE BICONE BRACELET

• A SIMPLE CHANGE OF BEAD COLOR and size along with a pattern variation

creates this thicker bracelet with more prominent square designs.

one · Attach the clasp in the same manner as for the green bracelet. Then thread one 4mm crystal and one seed bead onto each strand. Thread both wires in opposite directions through a 6mm crystal. String one more 6mm crystal onto each wire.

two · Thread both strands of wire in opposite directions through another 6mm crystal. Thread a seed bead onto each strand and repeat the pattern from the beginning. Finish as for the green and yellow bracelet.

flat pearl bracelet

MATERIALS

Finished Length: 7" (18cm), including clasp

9" (23cm) strand of .015 silver-plated stringing wire (Beadalon)

10 square freshwater pearls

5mm red (Siam), rose and crystal bicone beads (Swarovski)

2.75mm round silver spacer beads (Darice)

½" (1cm) silver head pins

silver-plated magnetic clasp (Beadalon)

no. 2 crimp tubes

round-nose pliers

crimping pliers

wire cutters

This feminine pearl bracelet brings a flash of pink and red sparkle into your day. Low-profile square pearls lay flat against your wrist while the little crystals swing playfully between them. The subtle coloring of the large pearls makes this bracelet perfect for both casual and dressy occasions.

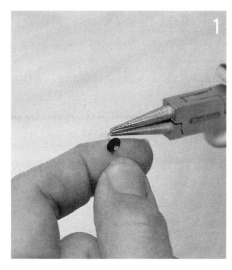

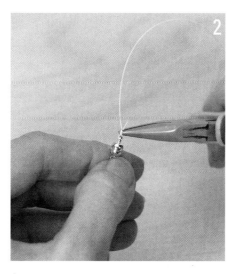

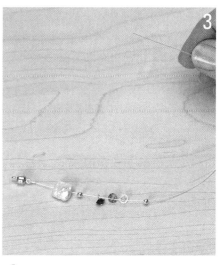

one · To begin, create all the dangles for the bracelet. Thread red, rose and crystal bicones on head pins and trim the head pin wire ¼" (61mm) above the last bead. Create a loop in the wire with round-nose pliers. Depending on the finished length of your bracelet, you should make nine dangles with each color bead (27 dangles total).

two · Use a no. 2 crimp tube to attach the magnetic clasp to a 9" (23cm) length of wire.

three · Begin stringing beads onto the wire in the following sequence: square pearl, spacer bead, three separate crystal dangles (one each of red, rose and crystal), spacer bead.

four · Repeat the beading pattern nine times or until you reach a finished length of 7" (18cm). Attach the other end of the clasp to the free end of the wire with a crimp tube.

ANOTHER SIMPLY BEAUTIFUL IDEA

These earrings use a single bead sequence from the bracelet—the only difference is that both the pearl and crystals hang from an eye pin. To make the earrings, thread an eye pin through the base of the square pearl. Shape the top of the eye pin and thread it through an earwire, then wrap it closed. Open the bottom loop of the eye pin and hook three wired crystals onto the loop. Reclose the eye pin loop, and the crystals should swing freely. Repeat for the second earring.

wired beads bracelet

MATERIALS

Finished Length: 7¾" (20cm), including clasp

wired beads (Blue Moon)

assorted glass beads in colors to match wired beads

1 brightly colored *E* bead

1" (3cm) sterling eye pins (Westrim)

sterling heart clasp (Darice)

6mm jump ring

round-nose pliers

chain-nose pliers

wire cutters

These beads come already wired, so it's a cinch to make this bracelet. Eye pins link easily through the wire loops on either end of the beads to quickly form a beaded chain. The silver heart clasp adds a fun-loving touch to the finished bracelet.

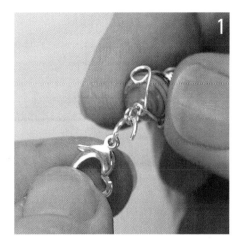

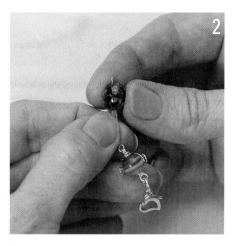

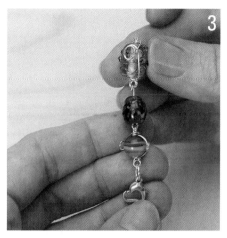

one · Link the clasp to the first wired bead in the bracelet with a jump ring (see Techniques, page 14).

two · Link the first wired bead to an eye pin loop and slide a non-wired bead onto the eye pin. Clip the eye pin wire to about ⅜" (1cm) above the bead with wire cutters.

three · Turn a loop in the eye pin wire and link another wired bead to it. Continue to link wired beads and non-wired beads on eye pins until you reach a total beaded length of 7½" (19cm).

four · Slide a small *E* bead onto a 6mm jump ring and link it to the final bead in the bracelet.

RINGS AND WIRE BRACELET

• THIS VARIATION USES JUMP RINGS THREADED WITH COLORFUL *E* BEADS TO CONNECT the wired beads into a bracelet. Always remember to open jump rings laterally (see Techniques, page 14) to help retain their shape.

To make this variation, simply link the wired beads together with beaded jump rings until you reach the total beaded length you like.

yellow turquoise bracelet

MATERIALS

Finished Length: 5¾" (15cm), including clasp

5 8½" (22cm) strands of .013 bright nylon-coated stringing wire (Beadalon)

4mm yellow turquoise rounds

silver seed beads

2 metal cones with flower imprint (Blue Moon)

small silver-plated pendant (Blue Moon)

2 2" (5cm) silver eye pins

10 no. 1 crimp tubes

3mm jump ring

toggle clasp (Darice)

round-nose pliers

crimping pliers

wire cutters

Beautiful stone beads are simply paired with silver cone ends and silver clasp to make this subtle bracelet. Look for long strands of polished stones in bead stores that will provide enough beads for five separate strands. Consider switching the beads to your favorite stones, such as colorful jaspers, black obsidian or translucent rose quartz.

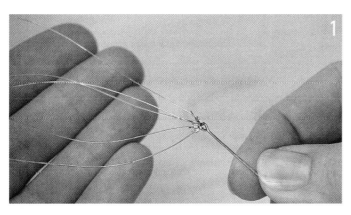

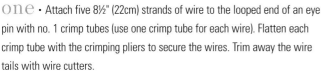

one · Attach five 8½" (22cm) strands of wire to the looped end of an eye pin with no. 1 crimp tubes (use one crimp tube for each wire). Flatten each crimp tube with the crimping pliers to secure the wires. Trim away the wire tails with wire cutters.

two · String five seed beads onto the beginning of each strand. (The seed beads will be hidden inside the cone ends when the bracelet is finished.) Continue beading the strands with the yellow turquoise rounds until the total beaded length reaches about 5¾" (15cm).

three · String five more seed beads onto the end of each wire and attach the wires to the loop end of the second eye pin with crimp tubes.

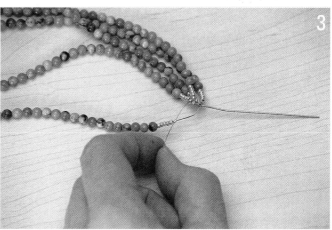

leftovers tip > See the earrings on page 100, where yellow turquoise beads are paired with carved stones to make unique earrings with your leftover beads.

four · Thread the eye pin through the cone and form a loop in the wire with round-nose pliers. Repeat on the other end of the bracelet.

five · Thread the circle end of the toggle onto the eye pin loop and wrap the tail of the wire around the base of the loop to secure it (see Techniques, page 16). Repeat with the bar end of the toggle clasp on the other side of the bracelet.

six · Attach the pendant to the toggle clasp loop with a jump ring.

stone, glass and pearl thirds bracelet

MATERIALS

Finished Length: 6¾" (17cm), including clasp

3 7½" (19cm) strands of .013 bright nylon-coated stringing wire (Beadalon)

12 adventurine stone chips (Blue Moon)

6 white freshwater pearls (Blue Moon)

10 green glass cubes

twisted silver beads

6 no. 1 silver crimp tubes

toggle clasp (Blue Moon)

crimping pliers

wire cutters

This bracelet consists of three straightforward beaded strands—what makes it interesting is the pairing of three different bead types in the center of each strand. The rough finish of the rock chips contrasts with both the smooth, round pearls and the perfect geometry of the green glass cubes. The subdued natural colors of green, orange and pearl help tie the three different elements together.

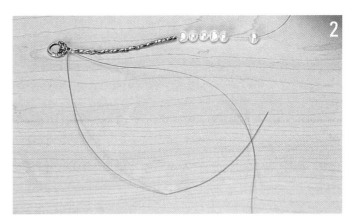

one · Attach three strands of wire to the circle end of the toggle clasp with a crimp tube. Thread the first strand with silver beads until you have beaded about 2¼" (6cm) of the strand.

two · Thread six pearls onto the strand.

three · Finish beading the first strand with 2¼" (6cm) of silver beads. Repeat for the other two strands, beading the center third of each of the remaining strands with 12 adventurine chips and ten green cubes, respectively. Bead the final 2¼" (6cm) of each of those strands with silver beads. Attach each strand to the bar end of the toggle clasp with a crimp tube.

THIRDS EARRINGS

● ORNATE POST EARRINGS AND DULL

CHAIN LENGTHS help these earrings

match both the decorative clasp and dark

silver twist beads in the bracelet.

one · Cut pieces of chain for each earring to the following lengths: two ¾" (2cm) pieces and four ½" (1cm) pieces. Slide two of each bead used in the center of the bracelet (pearls, green cubes and adventurine chips) onto head pins (six beaded head pins total). Cut the wire to about ⅜" (1cm) above each bead and turn a loop. Attach each beaded head pin to a ½" length of chain. Attach the pearl dangles to the ¾" (2cm) lengths of chain.

two · Attach the tops of the three chains to one jump ring. Attach the jump ring to a post earring, opening and closing it with round-nose pliers. Repeat to make the second earring.

color fall bracelet

MATERIALS

Finished Length: 8" (20cm), including clasp

6 10" (25cm) strands of .013 bright nylon-coated stringing wire (Beadalon)

assorted red glass beads (dark, medium and sandwashed red)

coral beads

deep red *E* beads

silver, medium and dark red seed beads

silver spacer beads (Blue Moon)

three-hole clasp (Blue Moon)

6 no. 3 crimp tubes

crimping pliers

wire cutters

tape

M y favorite summertime bracelet garners compliments wherever I go. The multiple strands feature a variety of red beads from coral to translucent glass, and the beaded lengths are twisted together so they cascade into a colorful river of beads. Simply amass a selection of beads in your favorite color to customize your own Color Fall Bracelet.

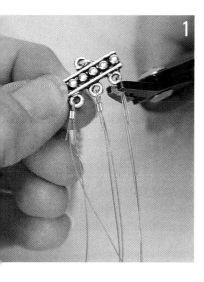
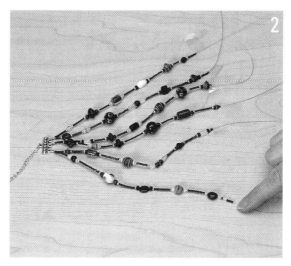

one · Attach two wires to each ring on the clasp using one crimp tube for each pair of wires. Double crimp the tubes with the crimping pliers (see Techniques, page 15). Trim away the excess wire tails with wire cutters.

two · String each strand with a random mix of beads, alternating between about 1" (3cm) of seed beads, silver spacer beads and coral beads and the following sequence: silver seed bead, *E* bead, glass bead, *E* bead, silver seed bead. Repeat the pattern and stagger it for each strand. As you finish beading, tape each end so the beads do not scatter.

three · Twist the strands so they are not laying straight. They should overlap each other.

four · Attach a mixed pair of strands to the other end of the clasp with crimp tubes.

ANOTHER SIMPLY BEAUTIFUL IDEA

In this Color Fall Bracelet, cool blue beads are paired with silver, white and clear glass accent beads. The strands sit closer together as they're narrowed at the ends to join the *O* ring and toggle clasp.

four strand bracelet

MATERIALS

Finished Length: 7" (18cm), including clasp

4 0½" (22cm) strands of .013 bright nylon-coated stringing wire (Beadalon)

10mm olive jade faceted cushion beads

8mm faceted red pearls

clear glass rectangle beads

2mm x 4mm silver metal spacer beads (Darice)

silver-lined clear *E* beads

silver and green seed beads

four-strand silver clasp with rhinestones

8 no. 1 crimp tubes

crimping pliers

wire cutters

tape

Red pearls, silver metal, cushion jade and clear glass rectangle beads are strung on separate wires to make the four distinctly different strands that come together in this bracelet. By placing small silver, clear and green seed beads between the larger beads, the strands begin to work together. The ornate rhinestone clasp is the final key in coordinating the four strands. The finished bracelet is so versatile, it pairs well with many outfits.

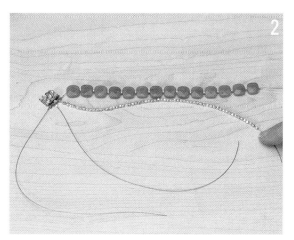

one · Attach four 8½" (22cm) wires to one end of a four-strand clasp with crimp tubes. Use crimping pliers to secure the wires. Trim the wire tails from the ends of the strands with wire cutters.

two · String the first strand, alternating between jade cushion beads and silver seed beads. String the second strand with silver metal spacer beads. The approximate beaded length should be about 6½" (17cm). As you finish beading a strand, tape the free end to secure the beads.

three · String the third strand, alternating between faceted red pearls and silver seed beads. String the final strand in the following sequence: glass rectangle, green seed bead, *E* bead, green seed bead. Bead both strands until the beaded length is about 6½" (17cm). Attach all four strands to the holes in the other end of the four-strand clasp with crimp tubes.

RED PEARL EARRINGS

• **THE RHINESTONE HEAD PINS COUPLED WITH ORNATE** bead caps make these earrings interesting from above and below. The earrings can be just as easily made with cushion jade beads—simply decide which of the bracelet beads to transform into earrings.

one · Thread a silver bead cap and a red faceted pearl onto a rhinestone head pin.

two · Turn a loop just above the bead and wrap the wire tail into a spiral that covers the top of the bead (see Techniques, page 17). Open the base of the earwire and thread the looped pearl onto the earring.

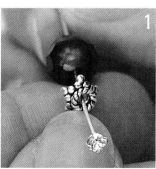

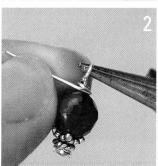

chained pearls bracelet

MATERIALS

Finished Length: 8" (20cm), including clasp

7" (18cm) of 2mm elongated silver-plated chain (Beadalon)

grey freshwater pearls (Blue Moon)

silver-plated lobster clasp (Beadalon)

2" (5cm) silver head pins

round-nose pliers

chain nose pliers

wire cutters

All in a row, each little pearl dangles from an individual chain link along the length of this bracelet. The blue-grey pearls complement and reflect the silver chain. Each pearl is tightly wrapped with wire, making the finished bracelet sturdy enough for everyday wear.

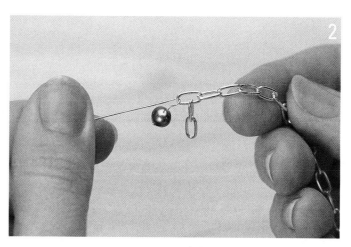

one • Slide a pearl bead onto a sterling silver head pin and shape it into an open loop at the top.

two • Slide the dangle onto a link in the chain. Use the round-nose pliers to wrap the wire several times around the base of the loop. Continue to wrap the wire tail, creating a spiral that partially covers the top of the bead in a decorative fashion (see Techniques, page 17).

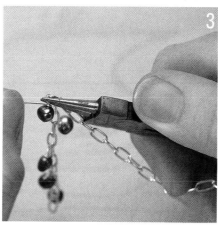

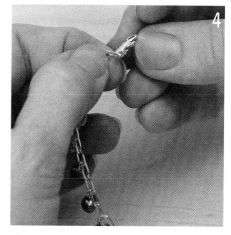

three • Continue to attach pearl dangles to every other link on the chain.

four • Attach the clasp to the end of the chain. Attach one final pearl dangle to the final link on the other end of the chain.

PEARL EARRINGS

• THESE FRESHWATER PEARLS ARE PERFECTLY sized to make pretty blue-grey clusters. These darling spring lever earrings make the perfect accent for the simple chain bracelet.

Slide three pearls onto head pins, cut the wire above them to about ⅜" (1cm) and create a wrapped loop above each pearl. (If you plan to make a wrapped loop or a spiral loop on top of the bead, don't cut the wire until the wrap is completed.) Open the loop on the earwire and slide all three dangles onto it. Close the earwire loop to finish, and repeat to make the second earring.

beads and baubles bracelet

MATERIALS

Finished Length: 8¾" (22cm), including clasp and extra chain link

8" (20cm) of medium wide silver-plated cable chain (Blue Moon)

assorted jade plastic beads (The Beadery)

rainbow seed beads

2" (5cm) silver-plated head pins

lobster clasp (Beadalon)

round-nose pliers

wire cutters

This chunky bracelet is deceptively lightweight—the large beads are plastic. Each series of beads is strung onto individual head pins that are hooked onto individual chain links, so they swing freely with every movement. The additional hanging chain length is both decorative and functional, making the finished bracelet size adjustable.

one • To begin making the bracelet, first prepare all the dangles you will be attaching to the bracelet. String different combinations of beads onto head pins in various lengths, making sure to string on a seed bead first (the seed beads will prevent the large-holed beads from falling off the wire). Cut the wire about ¼" to ⅜" (61mm to 1cm) above the bead or beads, depending on the size of the bead, and turn a loop in the wire. Attach the first beaded head pin four links in from one end of the 8" (20cm) length of chain.

two • Continue to attach beaded head pins to the links in the chain, sometimes skipping links and sometimes attaching multiple dangles to the same link. Leave 2" (5cm) of unbeaded chain (about 13 links) at the end of the bracelet.

three • Open the loop on the lobster clasp with round-nose pliers and slide it onto the first link in the length of chain.

four • At the other end of the chain, attach two decorative head pins beaded with small beads. This bracelet is adjustable, so the clasp can hook onto any of the 11 open links. Clasp it closer to the heavily beaded area for a tight fit, or by the two decorative head pins for a looser fit.

linked memory wire cuff

MATERIALS

bracelet memory wire

2 three-hole spacers

turquoise Japanese seed beads

shaped glass beads, seed beads and
E beads in turquoise, orange, peridot,
brown and green

turquoise miracle beads

round-nose pliers

chain-nose pliers

wire cutters

The center of this little cuff bracelet showcases a vibrant mixture of colors and bead varieties. Three separate coils of memory wire are cleverly joined at the sides with two separate three-hole spacers. The wire tension makes the bracelet adjustable and holds it firmly in place around your wrist.

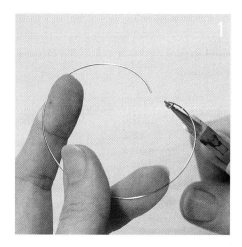

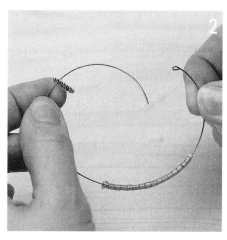

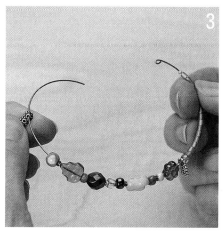

one · Allow the memory wire to coil around your wrist one time and cut a piece to fit. Cut two more pieces to the same length. Shape a loop at one end of each of the wires using round-nose pliers. Squeeze the loop flat with chain-nose pliers.

two · Thread one small seed bead followed by 15 Japanese seed beads onto one of the wires, and then one peridot *E* bead. Thread the wire through the first hole in a three-hole spacer.

three · String about one half of the total length of the memory wire with colorful glass beads, including one or a few turquoise miracle beads. Slide the wire through the first hole in a second three-hole spacer. String step two in reverse (peridot, 15 Japanese seed beads, one turquoise seed bead). Fold over the end of the memory wire as in step one.

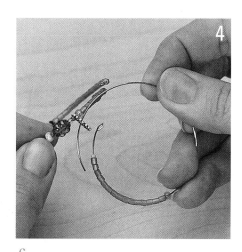

five · Continue to bead each piece of memory wire just as you beaded the first piece. Slide each length of memory wire through the second and third holes (respectively) of the three-hole spacer after beading the first quarter and after beading the center. Finish beading all the memory wire pieces and turn a small loop in the end of each one with round-nose and chain-nose pliers to finish.

four · String about one fourth of the second piece of memory wire with turquoise Japanese seed beads and one peridot *E* bead. Slide the wire through the second (or middle) hole in the first spacer on the beaded piece of memory wire.

stretchy eye pin bracelet

MATERIALS

Finished Length: 6¾" (17cm)

2 11" (28cm) strands of 1mm clear
elastic cord (Elasticity by Beadalon)

24 2" (5cm) silver-plated eye pins

brown Czech glass beadlettes

glass bead mix with flowers,
hearts and ovals (Blue Moon)

2 no. 4 crimp tubes

round-nose pliers

crimping pliers

wire cutters

G-S Hypo Cement

scissors

tape

You'll have no trouble wearing this comfortable brace-let on your wrist all day long. Charming flower- and heart-shaped glass beads are threaded onto eye pins to make vertical links. The links are strung together with heavyweight clear elastic, making the finished bracelet completely adjustable.

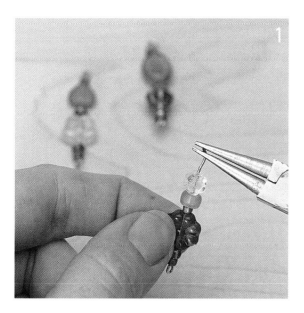

one · Begin the bracelet by making all the eye pin "beads." Cut the eye pins down to 1½" (4cm) each with wire cutters. Randomly string beads onto the eye pins, beading about 1¼" (3cm) of the eye pin length. Create a loop at the open end of the eye pin with round-nose pliers.

two · Tape one end of one piece of elastic. Alternate stringing beaded eye pins and brown glass beadlettes onto the length of elastic. Continue stringing until the finished length reaches about 6¾" (17cm).

three · Once all the beads and eye pins are strung onto the first elastic, thread the other piece of elastic, alternating between brown beadlettes and the bottom loop in the beaded eye pins.

four · Slide the ends of one strand through a no. 4 crimp tube in opposite directions so that they slide past each other inside the tube. Flatten the crimp tube with the crimping pliers to finish. Repeat to secure the ends of the other elastic strand. Apply a dab of G-S Hypo Cement to the elastic where it emerges from each crimp tube. Allow the adhesive to dry.

woven carved flower bracelet

MATERIALS

Finished Length: 7¼" (18cm), including clasp

3 11" (28cm) strands of .015 bright nylon-coated stringing wire (Beadalon)

carved stone flower bead (Blue Moon)

tan, brown and burgundy bugle bead, seed and *E* bead mix

no. 4 crimp tubes

leaf toggle clasp (Blue Moon)

crimping pliers

wire cutters

Three strands randomly strung with a mix of crimson, bronze and brown beads intersect at intervals to make an attractive web of loops in this bracelet. All three strands come together at both the clasp and at the carved rose bead, giving this piece a natural, organically flowing feel.

one · Attach the circle end of the toggle clasp to three 11" (28cm) strands of wire, securing them all through one no. 4 crimp tube. Double crimp the tube to secure the strands. String beads in a random pattern onto two strands for about 1" (3cm) of beads. Thread both strands through one E bead.

two · Bead one of the two beaded strands and the third strand with a random pattern of beads. When you have beaded to about 2½" (6cm) from the clasp, thread both of those strands through one E bead.

three · Continue beading the strands and threading two strands through one bead at random intervals. At the end of the bracelet, slide all three strands through a carved flower bead.

four · To finish the bracelet, attach the bar end of the toggle clasp with a no. 4 crimp tube. Double crimp the crimp tube with the crimping pliers to secure the clasp and finish the bracelet.

ANOTHER SIMPLY BEAUTIFUL IDEA

This woven-look necklace is made just like the bracelet. Continue beading and threading the strands in and out until you've added enough length to encircle your neck. The web-like pattern shows more clearly with the additional length in the necklace.

earrings

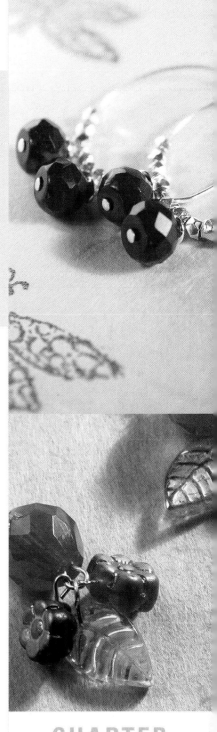

When you reach for earrings, you probably never stop to think how easy and inexpensive they are to make. And if quick and cheap aren't incentive enough, just think about how fun it is to create earrings in the colors and styles that suit you best. Having recently had my ears pierced for the first time, I relished the opportunity to create my own personalized earring wardrobe.

Earrings are the perfect way to showcase rare or expensive beads; unlike in a bracelet or necklace, the beads aren't hidden in multiple strands or lost in elaborate stringing patterns. Simply constructed of understated beads and metal jewelry findings, beaded earrings capture constant attention. And the biggest advantage is the savings—you only need to purchase two special beads to make stunning earrings.

Once you've mastered the simple earring-making techniques, you have the perfect gift-making skill at your fingertips. Before you know it, you'll be quickly threading eye pins and head pins through a myriad of different bead varieties to make original earring designs.

CHAPTER

3

red hoop earrings

MATERIALS

1" (3cm) sterling silver hoops

Bali beads

silver saucer beads

4 carved red stones

½" (1cm) silver head pins

round-nose pliers

wire cutters

Hoop earrings are a breeze to make—any bead slides easily onto the narrow wire. For added dimension, thread stone beads onto short head pins before adding them to the beaded hoops. The natural red stone beads used in these earrings are beautifully complemented by both the silver beads and the earring wires.

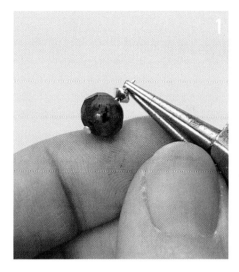

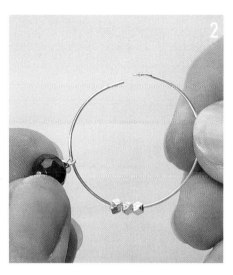

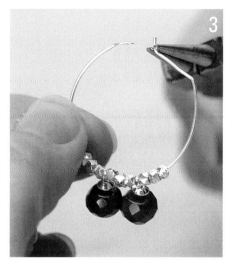

one · Slide a red stone bead and a silver saucer bead onto a head pin. Turn a loop in the head pin wire to create a dangle. Repeat to make one more dangle.

two · Slide three Bali beads onto the hoop, and then slide on the first red stone dangle.

three · Finish beading the hoop by threading on three more Bali beads, a red stone dangle and three more Bali beads. Bend the wire in about ½" (1cm) from the end to straighten the end of the hoop. Bend the very end of the hoop wire up at about a 45° angle so that it can slide easily into the hole on the other end of the hoop. Repeat to make the second earring.

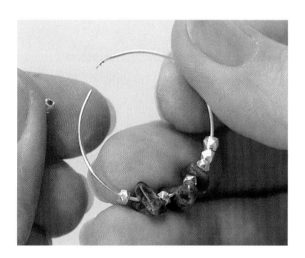

SLIDING BEADS HOOP EARRINGS

• S K I P   T H E   H E A D   P I N S   I N   T H I S   V A R I A T I O N , and thread rock chip beads directly onto the hoop earrings. Their irregular shape is the perfect contrast to small silver Bali beads.

To make this very simple variation, simply slide silver Bali beads and blue chip beads directly onto the hoop. Bend the very end of the hoop wire up at about a 45° angle so that it can slide easily into the hole on the other end of the hoop. Repeat to make the second earring.

stone and chain earrings

MATERIALS

silver earwires

2 1⅛" (3cm) lengths of
sterling cable chain

teardop carved fluorite stones

2 2" (5cm) silver eye pins

round-nose pliers

chain-nose pliers

wire cutters

The new beading trend in earring design has been to hang individual, pairs or small groups of beads from short lengths of chain. The appeal is easy to understand—the finished earrings swing playfully from your earlobes. The key to success is scaling the width and length of the chain to the beads. I selected heavier-weight chain to pair with these carved teardrop stones, rather than the fine chain used in the Chain Earrings on page 53. Experiment with different lengths of chain and bead varieties to find what works best for you.

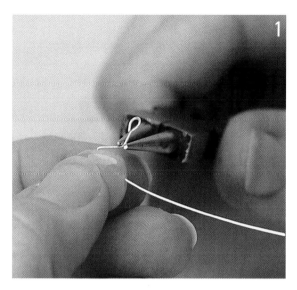

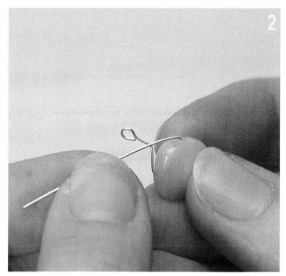

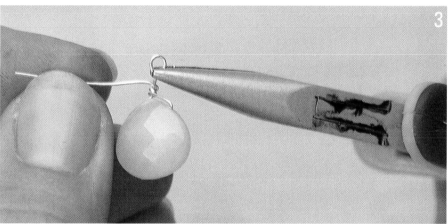

one · Slide the blue fluorite stone onto an eye pin and bend the loop end of the eye pin up to the top of the stone.

two · Bend the other end of the eye pin up to the top of the stone and bring it across the other end of the wire.

three · Wrap the tail end of the wire around the base of the eye pin loop several times to secure the stone. Trim away the excess wire with wire cutters.

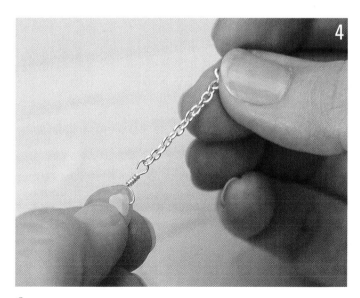

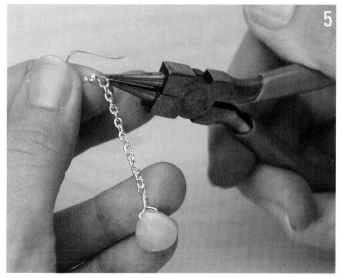

four · Open the eye pin loop and slide the dangle onto the last link of a 2" (5cm) section of chain. Close the link with round-nose and chain-nose pliers.

five · Attach the top link of the section of chain to an earwire loop and close the link with pliers. Repeat to make the matching earring.

flower bunch earrings

MATERIALS

lever back earwires

2 10mm faceted pink beads

2 each of the following glass beads: purple flower beads, small black flower beads, 12mm x 18mm iridescent leaf beads

4 silver eye pins

4½" (11cm) silver head pins

round-nose pliers

wire cutters

At first glance, the large faceted rose crystal beads in these earrings are what attract your attention. On closer inspection you'll discover the more subtle beauty of a delightful hanging bouquet of glass flower and leaf beads.

one · Thread a pink faceted bead onto an eye pin and make a loop at the top with round-nose pliers. Slide the loop onto the earwire and wrap the tail of the wire around the base of the loop (see Techniques, page 16). Trim off any excess wire tail with wire cutters.

two · Slide a flower bead onto a head pin and trim the wire to about ⅜" (1cm) above the bead. Make a small loop above the bead with round-nose pliers. Repeat with another flower bead.

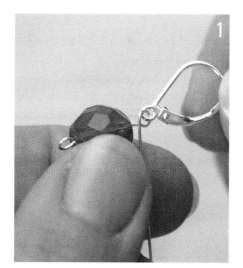
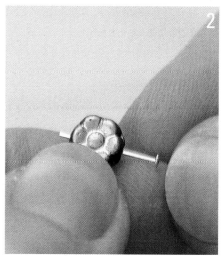

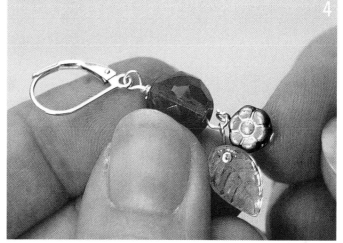

three · Slide a leaf bead onto a head pin and bend the head pin wire to a 90° angle. Create a loop in the top of the wire with round-nose pliers so that the head pin forms an S shape.

four · Attach both of the dangles to the eye pin loop on the pink faceted bead by opening and closing the loops with pliers. Repeat to make the second earring.

ANOTHER SIMPLY
BEAUTIFUL
IDEA

Change the appearance of the earrings by simply switching the bead color palette to green, black and white. If you're having trouble locating leaf and flower beads, substitute heart- and butterfly-shaped glass beads.

crystal cube earrings

MATERIALS

lever back earrings

8mm black diamond cubes (Swarovski)

4mm jet diagonal cubes (Swarovski)

silver head pins

silver eye pins

round-nose pliers

wire cutters

These elegant Swarovski crystal cubes are simply hung from plain silver head and eye pins. The cubes swing freely to playfully catch and refract light with each turn of your head.

one · Slide a black diamond cube bead onto a head pin and measure up about ¼" (61mm). Make a loop in the wire (see Techniques, page 16). Trim away the excess wire with wire cutters.

two · Slide an eye pin onto the open loop and then close it with round-nose pliers.

three · Slide a jet diagonal cube onto the eye pin.

four · Cut the eye pin wire to about ⅜" (1cm) above the bead and make a loop in the wire with round-nose pliers. Slide the loop onto the earwire and close the loop with pliers.

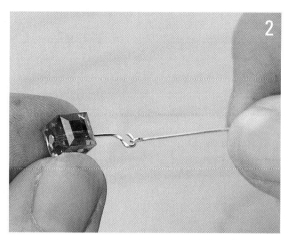

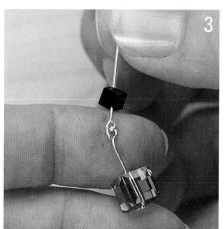

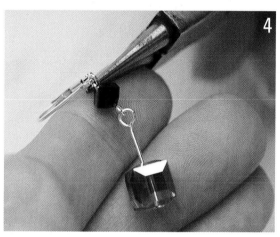

ANOTHER SIMPLY BEAUTIFUL IDEA

These intricately cut teardrops remind me of chandelier crystals. They've been simply paired with coordinating round crystals to make this elegant earring variation. To make the earrings, slide a jump ring through the hole in the teardrop and link the jump ring to the loop in the eye or head pin.

twisted leaf earrings

MATERIALS

sterling silver post earrings (Blue Moon)

8" (20cm) strand of 26-gauge sterling silver wire (Darice)

2 blue-grey freshwater pearls (Blue Moon)

4 iridescent glass leaf beads

round-nose pliers

wire cutters

These tiny flowering stems are easy to create—just twist folded sterling wires together with your fingertips. Fresh-water pearl buds and miniature glass leaves are simply threaded onto the wires and then twisted into place. The length of the stems is completely adjustable. If you prefer, make smaller earrings with a single bud and one or two leaves, or extend the stem and add more pearls and leaves to make a longer earring.

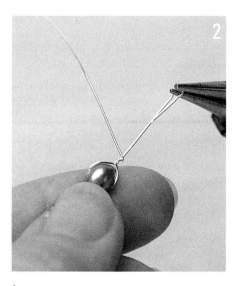

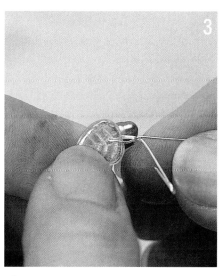

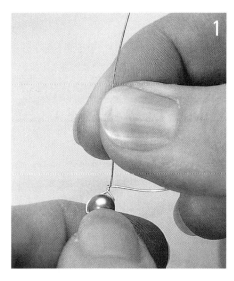

one · Cut about 8" (20cm) of wire and thread a freshwater pearl onto one end, about 2½" (6cm) or so from the end of the wire. Twist the wires together three times to secure the bead.

two · Measure up about ⅞" (2cm) from the top of the twisted bead and then wrap one wire around the round-nose pliers to make a small loop that is open at the bottom with about ½" (13mm) of straight wire under the loop. This wire will form the center stem.

three · Thread a leaf bead onto the open wire, hold the leaf ⅜" (1cm) away from the pearl, and fold the wire end back down toward the pearl. The leaf will be trapped on a wire loop. Then tightly twist the wire loop three times to create a short stem. Twist the wire three times around the central stem. Repeat to add two more leaves, separating each addition with three twists around the center stem wire.

four · Wrap the wire around the open end of the open loop shape to secure the opening.

five · Open the loop on the earring post and slide on the loop at the top of the twisted wire. Use pliers to close and secure the loop.

ANOTHER SIMPLY BEAUTIFUL IDEA

Freshwater pearls come in a wide range of colors. Select your favorite and then find coordinating glass leaf beads to match.

chandelier earrings

MATERIALS

earwires

silver chandelier forms

4 6mm crystal bicone beads (Swarovski)

4 5mm rose bicone beads (Swarovski)

2 9mm x 6mm rose teardop beads (Swarovski)

2 silver head pins

6 ½" (1cm) silver head pins

round-nose pliers

wire cutters

It's all in the name—just like in chandelier light fixtures, the loops in these silver frames are especially designed to hang beads. You'll find a wide range of frame styles in both bead and craft stores, many of which are both large and geometric. I prefer the comfortable size of this teardrop-shaped frame, which is enhanced by intricate metal detailing.

one · To make the center dangle, slide a rose teardrop bead and a 6mm bicone crystal onto a head pin. Cut the wirc to about ⅜" (1cm) above the bead and turn a loop in the wire above the bead with round-nose pliers.

two · Open the loop at the top of the center dangle and link it to the top center loop on the chandelier form. Close the loop with pliers.

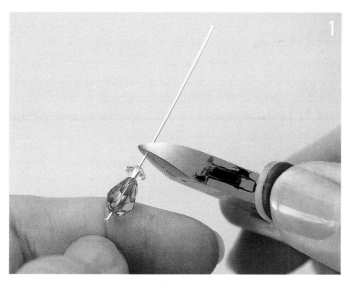

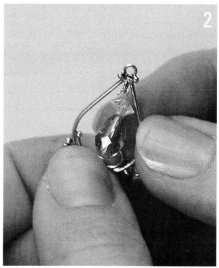

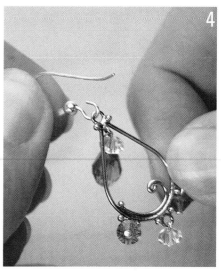

three · To make the tiny dangles that hang from the bottom loops on the chandelier form, slide 5mm rose and 6mm clear crystals onto ½" (1cm) head pins and trim the head pins to about ⅜" (1cm) above the beads. Turn loops in the wire of each dangle, attaching them to the loops at the bottom of the chandelier form as you do so.

four · To finish the earring, open the loop on the earwire with pliers and slide the loop on the chandelier form onto the earwire loop. Close the earwire loop with pliers to secure the chandelier form. Repeat to make the matching earring.

ANOTHER SIMPLY BEAUTIFUL IDEA

I used the identical chandelier frames to demonstrate how changing bead colors and shapes along with the type of earring findings alters the finished earring.

MATERIALS

gold earring posts (Blue Moon)

gold spacer beads (Blue Moon)

2 gold-plated head pins

2 grey freshwater pearls

2 7.5mm white glass pearls

round-nose pliers

wire cutters

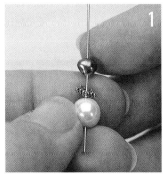

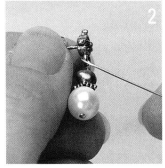

SEMIPRECIOUS EARRINGS

• **THESE EARRINGS ELEGANTLY PAIR TWO VARIETIES** of pearls with gold jewelry findings to make earrings equally suited for the workplace and for more formal occasions.

one • Thread a glass pearl, a gold spacer bead and a freshwater pearl onto a head pin and cut the head pin wire about ⅜" (1cm) above the beads. Turn a loop in the wire above the beads with round-nose pliers.

two • Attach the dangle to the earring post and spiral the wire end on top of the bead with round-nose pliers.

ANOTHER SIMPLY BEAUTIFUL IDEA

These ornate carved stone beads have been carefully paired with both small gold beads and yellow turquoise beads that complement the stones without drawing attention away from their intricate design.

MATERIALS

sterling silver large ball hook wire (CCA Corp.)

ball-end head pin (CCA Corp.)

2 eye pins

faceted rose quartz cushion beads

7mm pink freshwater pearls

round-nose pliers

wire cutters

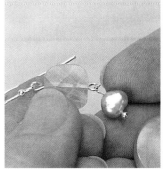

To make these earrings, slide a pink stone onto an eye pin, attach a freshwater pearl dangle to the loop and attach both stones to an earwire.

PINK DANGLE EARRINGS

• WHEN A SINGLE STONE JUST ISN'T ENOUGH, CONSIDER hanging graduated smaller stones from one larger bead. In this case, a beautiful matching pink-colored pearl hangs from a rose quartz stone. Individual eye pins allow the linked stones and pearls to move freely.

ANOTHER SIMPLY BEAUTIFUL IDEA

For a longer chain of stones, find coordinating faceted stone beads and link them together. Don't skip the pearl ending—you'll find them in every color.

accessories

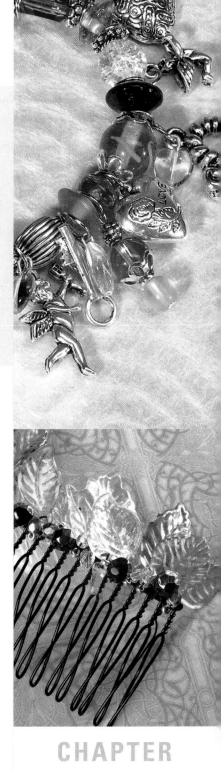

Beads usually play second fiddle to precious stones in the ring department, but beads bring a sparkle and whimsy to your fingertips that shouldn't be so quickly overlooked. The springy memory wire rings in this chapter were one of the most popular projects during the photography of this book—every time I turned around, someone else was playing dress up, sliding a ring onto her finger, turning her hand this way and that.

It's hard to resist playing dress up with beautiful beads. As someone who's always pulling my hair up into ponytails, I've often fallen prey to purchasing expensive beaded hair elastics. Once I set my mind to creating handmade versions, I was amazed how quickly and effortlessly both the rhinestone and beaded bauble elastics were assembled. In this chapter, you'll find other easy accessories to nestle beads in your hair, including leafy hair combs, beaded hair picks and headbands.

Wherever you go, whether at work or play, there are beaded accessories for every day of the week. Wrap a flowered beaded anklet around your foot before slipping on your sandals for a weekend in the sun. Brighten up your workday by transforming a necessity like a photo ID badge into an attractive necklace that's functional and beautiful. You're an experienced beader now—the options are virtually endless.

CHAPTER

4

elegant hair picks

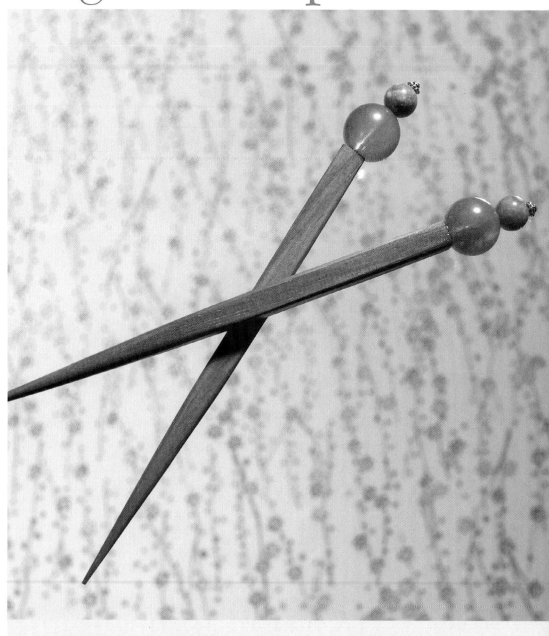

MATERIALS

4⅝" (12cm) wooden sticks with drilled hole (Beadin' Path)

2 2mm x 14mm polished rose quartz beads

2 8mm polished jasper beads

2 2" (5cm) decorative head pins (Blue Moon)

G-S Hypo Cement

wire cutters

By simply adding polished stone beads to the tops of wooden hair picks, you'll instantly create a sophisticated hair accessory. Twist shoulder-length hair into a loose topknot and thread the finished picks in opposite directions down through layers of hair to hold the hairstyle in place. Both beaded ends of the picks will emerge from the hair, lending an Asian flair to your upswept do.

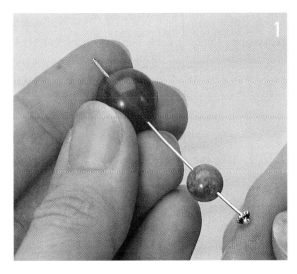

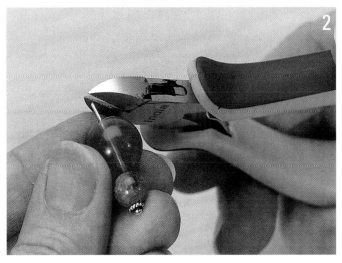

one · Slide a jasper bead and a rose quartz bead onto a decorative head pin.

two · Cut the head pin about ¼" (6mm) above the beads with wire cutters.

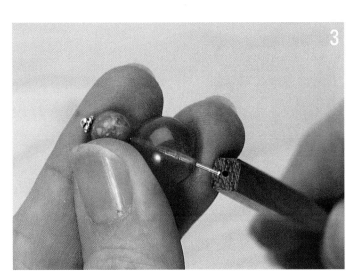

three · Squeeze some G-S Hypo Cement into the hole in the hairstick. Insert the head pin wire into the hole. Repeat to make a matching hairstick. Stake the wooden sticks upright in a glass, plant pot or piece of Styrofoam and let them dry overnight.

ANOTHER SIMPLY BEAUTIFUL IDEA

· The possible combinations of decorative head pins, polished stones and wooden sticks are endless. Test your design by first threading beads onto the head pin, and then holding it above the stick before trimming the pin and gluing it into place.

hair bauble

MATERIALS

coated hair elastic

plastic bead mix (The Beadery)

gold-plated head pins

6mm gold split ring

2 7mm gold-plated jump rings

round-nose pliers

chain-nose pliers

wire cutters

Next time you brush your hair into a ponytail, keep it in place with this playful cluster of beaded baubles. Made from plastic beads, the baubles are so lightweight you'll probably forget you're wearing them. If you like this bead variety, look up the Beads and Baubles Bracelet on page 78 that features the same beads in a different color and application.

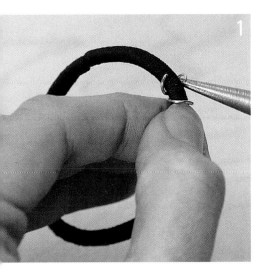

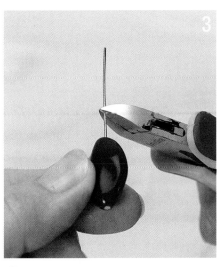

one · Open two 7mm gold jump rings with pliers and slide them onto a hair band (see Techniques, page 14).

two · Slide the split ring onto the open jump rings. Use pliers to close the jump rings and secure the split ring.

three · Slide beads onto head pins and cut the wire about ⅜" (1cm) above each bead. Use round-nose pliers to create a small loop above the beads (see Techniques, page 16).

four · Use pliers to open and close the loops on the beaded head pins and connect each one to the split ring. Continue connecting beaded head pins to the split ring until there are enough beads (about five to seven).

ANOTHER SIMPLY BEAUTIFUL IDEA

Perfect for blond hair, this neutral color variation uses lighter-colored beads and a beige coated hair elastic.

beaded headband

MATERIALS

silver metal headband

3' (91cm) strand of 32-gauge wire

½" (1cm) green stone beads

2mm sterling seed beads (Darice)

wire cutters

When you slide this lovely headband through your locks, you'll crown yourself with beautiful beads. This headband was created by tightly wiring green stone beads to a metal headband. The wire teeth thread through your hair so all that remains visible is a narrow band of beads.

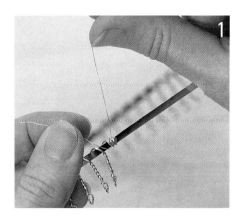

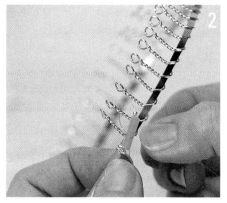

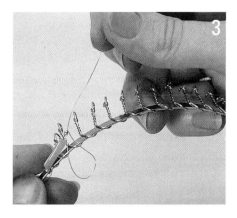

one • Cut about 3' (91cm) of wire and wrap one end tightly around one end of the headband to secure it. Thread a silver seed bead onto the wire and wrap the wire around the headband and back through the bead to secure it.

two • String a green stone bead and a silver seed bead onto the wire and wrap it behind the headband.

three • Bring the wire back to the front and through the silver seed bead again.

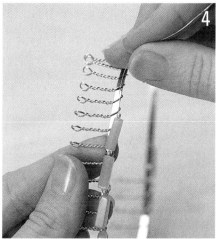

four • Continue beading the headband by stringing on an aventurite bead and a silver seed bead and bringing the wire behind the headband and back through each silver bead a second time.

five • Wrap the wire tightly around the end of the headband to secure it.

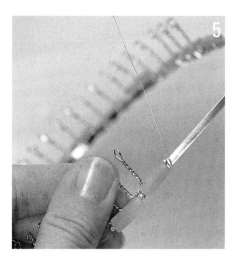

ANOTHER SIMPLY BEAUTIFUL IDEA

Perfect for dark hair, these deep brown stones shimmer with lustrous shades of ochre. The stones are separated by gold seed beads, which pick up the natural highlights in the stone beads.

leafy hair comb

MATERIALS

3" (8cm) black wire hair comb (Scünci)

34" (86cm) strand of 26-gauge black wire (Darice)

blue, purple and green leaf bead mix (Blue Moon)

4mm sapphire and violet fire-polished crystal beads (Darice)

6mm black fire-polished crystal beads (Darice)

silver seed beads

wire cutters

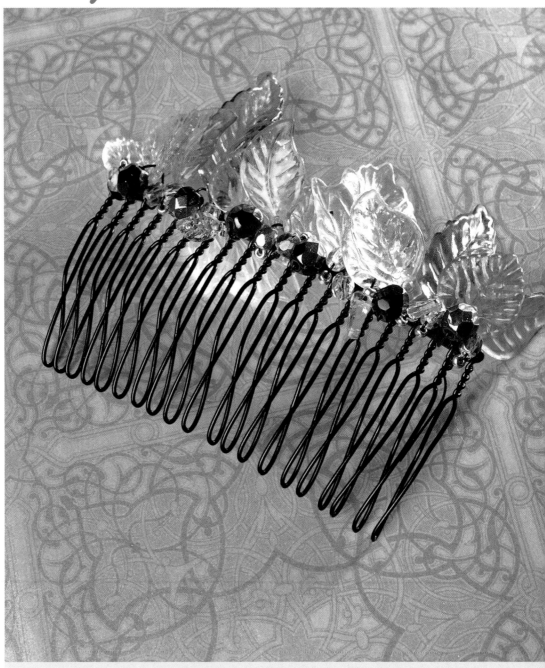

Brush your hair into an upswept style and hold it in place with this ephemeral hair comb. Sparkling fire-polished beads and colorful translucent leaves are intertwined around the top of a plain hair comb to transform it into a unique hair accessory.

one • Wrap one end of the wire around the hair comb and then twist the short end around the longer length to secure it.

two • Pull the wire from the back of the comb toward the front. Thread both a leaf bead and a fire-polished crystal bead onto the wire and slide them down so they rest against the top of the hair comb. Tightly wrap the wire from front to back around the comb.

three • Continue to thread leaf beads, fire-polished crystals and seed beads onto the wire and wrap the wire around the comb between the teeth to secure them.

four • When you are finished wrapping beads around the comb, make sure the wire is at the back of the comb and twist the tail around the comb to secure.

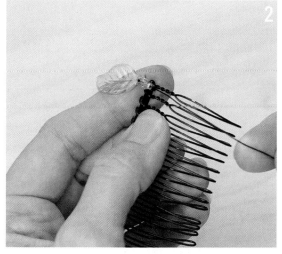

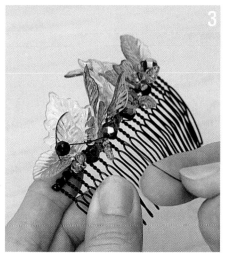

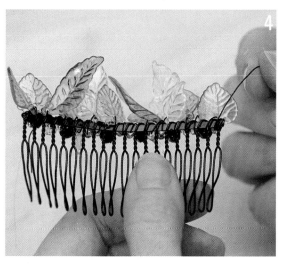

ANOTHER SIMPLY BEAUTIFUL IDEA

Rich autumn colors with undercurrents of gold seed beads make this earthy variation the perfect accent to any autumn color scheme. Besides changing the colors of the beads, consider switching the metal finish of the comb itself to match the hair color of the recipient—gold for blond, brown for brunette or silver for grey.

wedding tip > These combs are the perfect custom accessory for formal occasions, even weddings. Collect an assortment of beads, from large leaf- or flower-shaped beads to small seed beads, that complement your dress. Follow the steps to wire your selection onto a purchased hair comb.

rhinestone hair elastic

MATERIALS

coated hair elastic

18" (46cm) strand of 32-gauge beading wire

square rhinestone double-hole slider bead (Pure Allure)

4mm iridescent black fire-polished crystal beads (Darice)

2 4mm silver filigree beads (Darice)

wire cutters

Next time you pull your hair up into a ponytail, don't reach for the same old tired elastic. Take a few minutes to wire beautiful rhinestones and crystal beads onto a hair elastic, and customize your own unique hair accessory. The next time you pull up your hair, you can top off your look with a little sparkle.

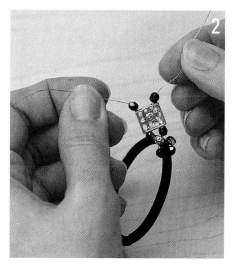

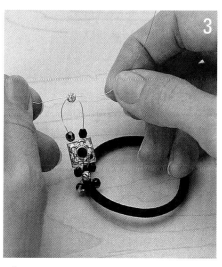

one · String three fire-polished crystals onto 18" (46cm) of wire. Let the beads fall to the center of the wire and hold the beads to the underside of the elastic. Bring the wire around to the front of the hair elastic and thread both ends of the wire through a silver filigree bead in opposite directions, tightening the loop of beads around the elastic.

two · Thread a fire-polished crystal onto each wire and then thread each wire through a set of holes in the rhinestone slider bead. Thread on two more crystals on the other side of the slider bead.

three · Thread both wire ends in opposite directions through another silver filigree bead.

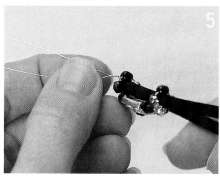

four · Thread one more fire-polished crystal onto each wire and then wrap the wires under the elastic. Thread both wires through another fire-polished crystal in opposite directions.

five · Feed both wires back through the entire beaded sequence, and when you get back to the beginning, twist the ends of the wires together to secure them.

ANOTHER SIMPLY BEAUTIFUL IDEA

Look for a wide choice of flat silver slider beads studded with colored rhinestones in craft stores. Pair the rhinestone slider with matching crystals and silver beads to adapt the pattern to your selection.

french flower bobby pins

MATERIALS

bobby pins

14" (36cm) strand of 26-gauge wire

dusty rose color mix seed beads

sandwashed red E bead

wire cutters

L ift your spirits with these fanciful beaded flowers— just slide the bobby pin ends into your hair and let the beaded blossoms adorn your locks. Guaranteed to never fade or wilt, all the care these sunny blossoms will ever need is a little pinch to reshape their petals.

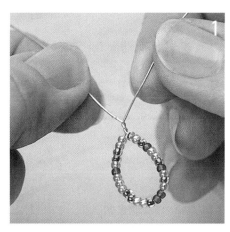

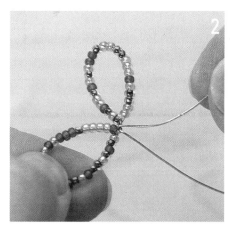

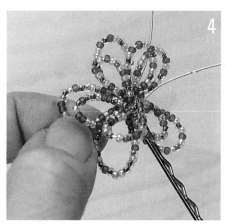

one · String about ¾" (2cm) of seed beads (about 25 beads) onto a 14" (36cm) piece of wire and form it into a loop. Twist the short wire around the long tail to secure the loop.

two · Create a second loop in the same manner, making a second twist next to the first twist to secure the loop.

three · Finish creating the flower by making three more loops. When the flower is done, slide a bobby pin onto the wire.

four · Construct a smaller flower on top of the first flower by making five smaller ½" (1cm) beaded loops with 19 seed beads wrapped in the center. The bobby pin will be secured between the two flower layers.

five · Bring both wires around to the front and bring the ends of both wires through a red *E* bead in opposite directions.

six · Turn the flower over and bring the ends of the wire to the back. Twist the wire ends together to secure them and then trim the tails.

ANOTHER SIMPLY BEAUTIFUL IDEA

A true-blue variation, like its namesake this forget-me-not flower begs to be remembered and worn daily—it's perfect with blue jeans.

chunky beads badge holder

MATERIALS

Finished Length: 30" (76cm), including badge holder

32" (81cm) strand of .018 nylon coated stringing wire (Beadalon)

badge holder (Blue Moon)

red, white and black matte glass bead mix (Blue Moon)

metallic bead mix (Blue Moon)

silver seed beads

matte white *E* beads

no. 2 crimp tube

crimping pliers

wire cutters

I designed this badge holder with my friend Lea Ann, who works for a national airline carrier, in mind. She had explained to me that whatever she wears needs to be durable enough to withstand getting accidentally snagged by luggage. If you're employed in a traditional office setting or healthcare facility, you might not share these concerns. Adjust the design by simply downgrading the weight of the stringing wire, and switch to lighter beads.

one · To begin the badge holder, string on a metallic bead, a red, white or black matte glass bead and another metallic bead. Alternate the first sequence with a pattern of seed bead, *E* bead, matte glass bead, *E* bead, seed bead. The pattern can be random—just let the larger matte beads set the rhythm.

two · When you reach about half of the desired finished beaded length, you'll create a loop where a badge or eyeglasses can be clipped on. Begin to create the loop by stringing on beads in the following sequence: metallic bead, matte glass bead, metallic bead, five seed beads, round metallic bead, badge holder.

three · Finish the loop by threading on another metallic bead and five seed beads. Thread the wire back through the first three beads in the sequence (metallic bead, matte glass bead, metallic bead).

four · Continue beading the remaining half of the badge holder in the same pattern as the first half. At the end of the badge holder, thread both ends of the wire in opposite directions through a no. 2 crimp tube and flatten and fold it to secure.

utilitarian tip > Of the many varieties of badge holders on the market, I found this design not only attractive but exceptionally useful. The badge clips onto the round end of the holder. Once you remove the badge you can thread one arm of your folded eyeglasses through the opening, a handy way to keep track of your spectacles when they're not in use.

blue flowering anklet

MATERIALS

Finished Length: 9" (23cm), including clasp

12" (30cm) strand of .015 nylon-coated stringing wire (Beadalon)

millefiori glass cane beads (The Beadery)

blue seed beads

2 no. 1 crimp tubes (Beadalon)

sterling lobster clasp (Darice)

4mm jump ring

crimping pliers

wire cutters

Whether you're at the beach or in town, circling your ankle with this ring of flowering beads will brighten your day. The seed beads are carefully chosen to blend with the colors of the millefiori glass cane beads. If you're having trouble locating the glass cane beads, you might consider substituting polymer clay beads that feature the same kind of flower patterns.

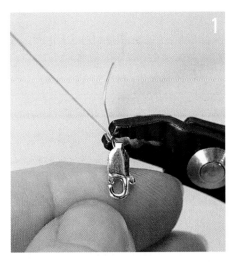

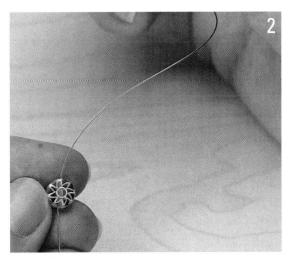

one · Attach a 12" (30cm) strand of wire to a lobster clasp with a crimp tube. Flatten the crimp tube with crimping pliers to secure it.

two · String ten seed beads followed by a millefiori glass cane bead onto the wire.

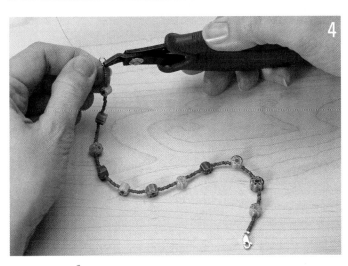

three · Continue beading in the established pattern until the final beaded length totals about 8¾" (22cm).

four · Attach a jump ring to the other end of the wire with a crimp tube (see Techniques, page 14). Trim away the excess wire to finish.

ANOTHER SIMPLY BEAUTIFUL IDEA

This more subtle variation features a melody of tan, rust and brown flowers that complements almost any skin tone.

brown memory wire ring

MATERIALS

ring memory wire coils

9mm x 6mm teardrop crystals: 1 violet,
2 topaz, 2 tanzanite (Swarovski)

violet, gold, amber, tan and
off-white seed beads

off-white E beads

5 silver head pins

4mm jump ring

round-nose pliers

chain-nose pliers

wire cutters

These tempting rings are actually miniature versions of the more commonly found memory wire bracelet. With these easy-to-make rings, the trickiest step is folding over the rigid wire ends. Both threading on the beads and attaching the crystal bead cluster are a snap.

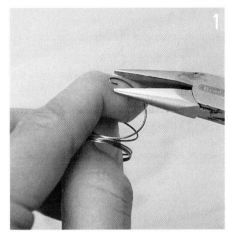

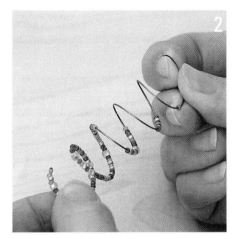

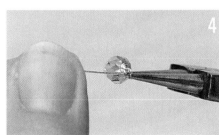

one • Cut about four and a half coils of ring memory wire. Use round-nose pliers to turn a small loop at one end of the ring. Use chain-nose pliers to flatten the loop.

two • String the coils with random beads in shades of brown and off-white until all the coils are beaded.

three • Use round-nose pliers to turn a small loop at the end of the ring and chain-nose pliers to close it tightly.

four • Thread a head pin through the narrow end of a teardrop crystal. Turn a loop at the top of the bead and make a spiral with the wire at the top of the bead. Repeat with the remaining crystals.

five • Link a 4mm jump ring to the top loop of the ring. Slide the bead dangles onto the jump ring. Pinch the jump ring closed.

*mixing tip > Having trouble finding the perfect bead mix? Just create your own by pouring small amounts of coordinating colored seed beads into a dish. You can influence the appearance of a bead mix by adding a larger quantity of deep-colored beads to make a dark mix, or, conversely, add a larger quantity of light-colored beads to make a lighter mix.

ANOTHER SIMPLY BEAUTIFUL IDEA

Turn your beads on their heads in this variation. Not only have the colors changed to purple, the crystals have been wired upside down. This unexpected twist changes the appearance of the finished crystal cluster.

woven seed bead ring

MATERIALS

28" (71cm) strand of 6-lb. size D FireLine thread (The Beadsmith)

silver-lined pink bugle beads

turquoise luster seed beads

2 size 12 sharp beading needles

G-S Hypo Cement

Although reminiscent of Native American beadwork, these woven rings are much easier to make and don't require a beading loom. Their low profile makes them comfortable to wear. The key to successfully stringing them is the FireLine beading thread. Lightweight yet strong, the strand threads easily through beading needles and has no trouble passing multiple times through a small seed bead.

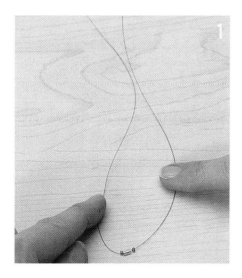 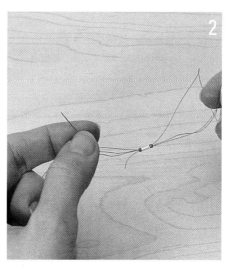 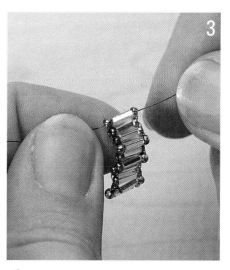

one · Cut a 28" (71cm) length of FireLine and thread a beading needle onto each end. String one turquoise seed bead, a pink bugle bead and another turquoise seed bead onto the center of the wire.

two · Slide on another row of beads and bring both ends of the wire through all the beads in opposite directions.

three · Repeat steps one and two to continue building the ring. Continue until you have a finished beaded length of 2¼" (6cm), or enough beading to wrap around the desired finger.

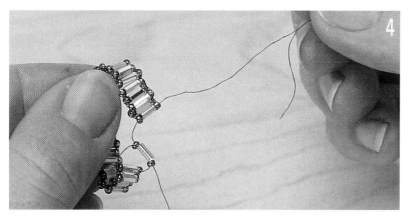 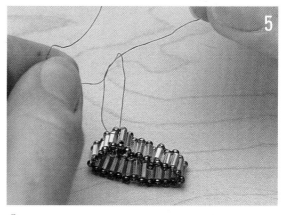

four · To make a circle, bring both ends of the ring together and thread the beading needle in the opposite direction through the first row of beads.

five · Tie the ends of the thread in a strong knot to secure the ring.

ANOTHER SIMPLY BEAUTIFUL IDEA

There is no end to the possible color and bead combinations that can be used in these little rings. These variations use seed and/or *E* beads—simply use more beads to make a wider band and fewer for a thinner band.

charm watch

MATERIALS

Finished Length: 6" (15cm)

12" (30cm) strand of 1mm clear beading elastic (Elasticity by Beadalon)

22mm x 24mm simple silver watch face (Darice)

12mm silver cast oval beads (Darice)

silver spacer beads (Darice)

10mm silver bead caps (Darice)

silver heart and cupid charm assortments (Darice, Blue Moon)

pink, light green and clear glass beads

1" (3cm) head pins

7mm jump rings

no. 4 crimp tubes

crimping pliers

round-nose pliers

scissors

A fun-loving timekeeper, this playful watch is drip-ping with sentiment. Whimsical heart, cupid and key charms along with glass and metal beads have been wired, connected with jump rings or strung around the watchband. Since it's made with heavyweight elastic, you won't have to struggle with a clasp—simply pull the finished bracelet over your hand for a comfortable fit.

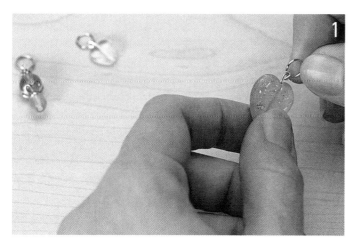

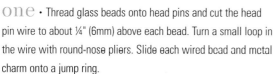

one • Thread glass beads onto head pins and cut the head pin wire to about ¼" (6mm) above each bead. Turn a small loop in the wire with round-nose pliers. Slide each wired bead and metal charm onto a jump ring.

two • Attach one side of the watch face to a piece of thick beading elastic with a no. 4 crimp tube. Use crimping pliers to flatten the crimp tube.

three • Slide a few charms randomly onto the elastic.

four • Slide on more beads following the charms. Continue stringing on beads and charms until the total beaded length is about 6" (15cm).

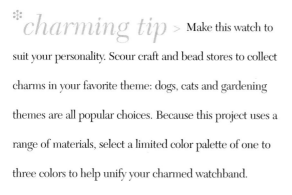

five • Secure the end of the elastic to the watch face with a no. 4 crimp tube. Flatten the crimp tube and trim away any excess elastic tail with scissors.

*charming tip > Make this watch to suit your personality. Scour craft and bead stores to collect charms in your favorite theme: dogs, cats and gardening themes are all popular choices. Because this project uses a range of materials, select a limited color palette of one to three colors to help unify your charmed watchband.

resources

CCA CORP.

www.cousin.com

* *glass pearls, AB faceted crystal coin mix, flat AB glass mix—turquoise and blue, fine silver chain, ball earring wires, ball-end head pins*

BEADALON

www.beadalon.com

* *stringing wires, Elasticity, chain-nose pliers, wire cutters, needle-nose pliers, memory wire, magnetic clasps, lobster clasps, elongated chain, crimp beads, crimp tubes*

DARICE

www.darice.com

* *glass beads, fire-polished beads, silver spacer beads, flower spacers, heart clasps, lobster clasps, O ring and toggle clasp, hook and eye clasp, earring findings, heart and cupid charms, silver watch face, 26-gauge silver wire*

THE BEADERY

www.thebeadery.com

* *Japanese seed beads, hair picks*

PURE ALLURE INC.

* *rhinestone slider beads, rhinestone plume, rhinestone clasp*

THE BEADIN' PATH

www.beadinpath.com

* *plastic beads, millefiori beads*

SWAROVSKI

* *crystals beads: cube, bicone, rounds, teardrop*

THE BEADSMITH

www.beadsmith.com

* *FireLine®*

TOOLSGS

www.toolsgs.com

* *G-S Hypo Cement*

BLUE MOON BEADS

www.bluemoonbeads.com

* *Czech glass beads, etched beads, glass flower beads, Summer Splash bead mix, wired beads, freshwater pearls, carved stone beads, carved rose beads, seed beads, spacer beads, earring findings, decorative head pins, badge holders, three- and four-strand clasps, ornate O ring and toggle clasps, lobster clasps, heart charms, sterling silver and plated chains, two-hole spacers, ornate three-hole spacers*

WESTRIM

www.westrimcrafts.com

* *32-gauge beading wire, Dazzle berry beads*